How Highly Effective People Speak

Eloquence

How Legendary Leaders Speak

Influential Leadership

Public Speaking Mastery

The 7 Keys to Confidence

Trust is Power

Influence

Decoding Human Nature

The Psychology of Persuasion

How Visionaries Speak

The Eloquent Leader

The Language of Leadership

The Psychology of Communication

The Charisma Code

Available on Amazon

Claim These Free Resources that Will Help You Unleash the Power of Your Words and Speak with Confidence. Visit www.speakforsuccesshub.com/toolkit for Access.

18 Free PDF Resources

30 Free Video Lessons

2 Free Workbooks

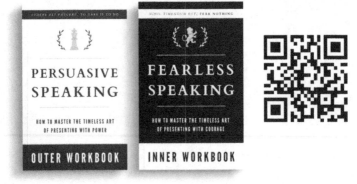

Claim These Free Resources that Will Help You Unleash the Power of Your Words and Speak with Confidence. Visit www.speakforsuccesshub.com/toolkit for Access.

18 Free PDF Resources

12 Iron Rules for Captivating Story, 21 Speeches that Changed the World, 341-Point Influence Checklist, 143 Persuasive Cognitive Biases, 17 Ways to Think On Your Feet, 18 Lies About Speaking Well, 137 Deadly Logical Fallacies, 12 Iron Rules For Captivating Slides, 371 Words that Persuade, 63 Truths of Speaking Well, 27 Laws of Empathy, 21 Secrets of Legendary Speeches, 19 Scripts that Persuade, 12 Iron Rules For Captivating Speech, 33 Laws of Charisma, 11 Influence Formulas, 219-Point Speech-Writing Checklist, 21 Eloquence Formulas

30 Free Video Lessons

We'll send you one free video lesson every day for 30 days, written and recorded by Peter D. Andrei. Days 1-10 cover authenticity, the prerequisite to confidence and persuasive power. Days 11-20 cover building self-belief and defeating communication anxiety. Days 21-30 cover how to speak with impact and influence, ensuring your words change minds instead of falling flat. Authenticity, self-belief, and impact – this course helps you master three components of confidence, turning even the most high-stakes presentations from obstacles into opportunities.

2 Free Workbooks

We'll send you two free workbooks, including long-lost excerpts by Dale Carnegie, the mega-bestselling author of *How to Win Friends and Influence People* (5,000,000 copies sold). *Fearless Speaking* guides you in the proven principles of mastering your inner game as a speaker. *Persuasive Speaking* guides you in the time-tested tactics of mastering your outer game by maximizing the power of your words. All of these resources complement the Speak for Success collection.

THE

LANGUAGE

OF

LEADERSHIP

HOW GREAT LEADERS USE THE LAWS OF POWERFUL LANGUAGE TO GET RESULTS

Peter Andrei

THE
LANGUAGE
OF
LEADERSHIP

SPEAK FOR SUCCESS COLLECTION BOOK

XIII

SPEAK
TRUTH
WELL
PRESS

A SUBSIDIARY OF SPEAK TRUTH WELL LLC
800 Boylston Street
Boston, MA 02199

**SPEAK
TRUTH
WELL LLC**

SPEAK FOR SUCCESS COLLECTION

Printed in the United States of America
40 39 38 37 36 35 34 33 32 31

While the author has made every effort to provide accurate internet addresses at the time of publication, neither the publisher nor the author assumes any responsibility for errors, or for changes that occur after publication. Further, the publisher does not have any control over and does not assume any responsibility for author or third-party websites or their content.

www.speakforsuccesshub.com/toolkit

FREE RESOURCES FOR OUR READERS

We believe in using the power of the internet to go above and beyond for our readers. That's why we created the free communication toolkit: 18 free PDF resources, 30 free video lessons, and even 2 free workbooks, including long-lost excerpts by Dale Carnegie, the mega-bestselling author of *How to Win Friends and Influence People*. (The workbooks help you put the most powerful strategies into action).

We know you're busy. That's why we designed these resources to be accessible, easy, and quick. Each PDF resource takes just 5 minutes to read or use. Each video lesson is only 5 minutes long. And in the workbooks, we bolded the key ideas throughout, so skimming them takes only 10 minutes each.

Why give so much away? For three reasons: we're grateful for you, it's useful content, and we want to go above and beyond. Questions? Feel free to email Peter directly at pandreibusiness@gmail.com.

www.speakforsuccesshub.com/toolkit

WHY DOES THIS HELP YOU?

I

The PDF resources cover topics like storytelling, logic, cognitive biases, empathy, charisma, and more. You can dig deeper into the specific topics that interest you most.

II

Many of the PDF resources are checklists, scripts, example-compilations, and formula-books. With these practical, step-by-step tools, you can quickly create messages that work.

III

With these free resources, you can supplement your reading of this book. You can find more specific guidance on the areas of communication you need to improve the most.

IV

The two workbooks offer practical and actionable guidance for speaking with complete confidence (*Fearless Speaking*) and irresistible persuasive power (*Persuasive Speaking*).

V

You can even learn from your phone with the free PDFs and the free video lessons, to develop your skills faster. The 30-lesson course reveals the secrets of building confidence.

VI

You are reading this because you want to improve your communication. These resources take you to the next level, helping you learn how to speak with power, impact, and confidence. We hope these resources make a difference. They are available here:

www.speakforsuccesshub.com/toolkit

From the desk of Peter Andrei
Speak Truth Well LLC
800 Boylston Street
Boston, MA 02199
pandreibusiness@gmail.com

May 15, 2021

What is Our Mission?

To whom it may concern:

The Wall Street Journal reports that public speaking is the world's biggest fear – bigger than being hit by a car. According to Columbia University, this pervasive, powerful, common phobia can reduce someone's salary by 10% or more. It can reduce someone's chances of graduating college by 10% and cut their chances of attaining a managerial or leadership position at work by 15%.

If weak presentation kills your good ideas, it kills your career. If weak communication turns every negotiation, meeting, pitch, speech, presentation, discussion, and interview into an obstacle (instead of an opportunity), it slows your progress. And if weak communication slows your progress, it tears a gaping hole in your confidence – which halts your progress.

Words can change the world. They can improve your station in life, lifting you forward and upward to higher and higher successes. But they have to be strong words spoken well: rarities in a world where most people fail to connect, engage, and persuade; fail to answer the question "why should we care about this?"; fail to impact, inspire, and influence; and, in doing so, fail to be all they could be.

Now zoom out. Multiply this dynamic by one thousand; one million; one billion. The individual struggle morphs into a problem for our communities, our countries, our world. Imagine the many millions of paradigm-shattering, life-changing, life-saving ideas that never saw the light of day. Imagine how many brilliant convictions were sunk in the shipyard. Imagine all that could have been that failed to be.

Speak Truth Well LLC solves this problem by teaching ambitious professionals how to turn communication from an obstacle into an engine: a tool for converting "what could be" into "what is." There is no upper limit: inexperienced speakers can become self-assured and impactful; veteran speakers can master the skill by learning advanced strategies; masters can learn how to outperform their former selves.

We achieve our mission by producing the best publications, articles, books, video courses, and coaching programs available on public speaking and communication, and at non-prohibitive prices. This combination of quality and accessibility has allowed Speak Truth Well to serve over 70,000 customers in its year of launch alone (2021). Grateful as we are, we hope to one day serve millions.

Dedicated to your success,

Peter Andrei
President of Speak Truth Well LLC
pandreibusiness@gmail.com

PROLOGUE:

This three-part prologue reveals my story, my work, and the practical and ethical principles of communication. It is not a mere introduction. It will help you get more out of the book. It is a preface to the entire 15-book Speak for Success collection. It will show you how to use the information with ease, confidence, and fluency, and how to get better results faster. If you would like to skip this, flip to page 50, or read only the parts of interest.

I

page XIII

MY STORY AND THE STORY OF THIS COLLECTION

how I discovered the hidden key to successful communication, public speaking, influence, and persuasion

II

page XXIV

THE 15-BOOK SPEAK FOR SUCCESS COLLECTION

confidence, leadership, charisma, influence, public speaking, eloquence, human nature, credibility - it's all here

III

page XXIX

THE PRACTICAL TACTICS AND ETHICAL PRINCIPLES

how to easily put complex strategies into action and how to use the power of words to improve the world

MY STORY AND THE STORY OF THIS COLLECTION

how I discovered the hidden key to successful communication, public speaking, influence, and persuasion (by reflecting on a painful failure)

HOW TO GAIN AN UNFAIR ADVANTAGE IN YOUR CAREER, BUSINESS, AND LIFE BY MASTERING THE POWER OF YOUR WORDS

I WAS SITTING IN MY OFFICE, TAPPING A PEN against my small wooden desk. My breaths were jagged, shallow, and rapid. My hands were shaking. I glanced at the clock: 11:31 PM. "I'm not ready." Have you ever had that thought?

I had to speak in front of 200 people the next morning. I had to convince them to put faith in my idea. But I was terrified, attacked by nameless, unreasoning, and unjustified terror which killed my ability to think straight, believe in myself, and get the job done.

Do you know the feeling?

After a sleepless night, the day came. I rose, wobbling on my tired legs. My head felt like it was filled with cotton candy. I couldn't direct my train of thoughts. A rushing waterfall of unhinged, self-destructive, and meaningless musings filled my head with an uncompromising cacophony of anxious, ricocheting nonsense.

"Call in sick."

"You're going to embarrass yourself."

"You're not ready."

I put on my favorite blue suit – my "lucky suit" – and my oversized blue-gold wristwatch; my "lucky" wristwatch.

"You're definitely not ready."

"That tie is ugly."

"You can't do this."

The rest went how you would expect. I drank coffee. Got in my car. Drove. Arrived. Waited. Waited. Waited. Spoke. Did poorly. Rushed back to my seat. Waited. Waited. Waited. Got in my car. Drove. Arrived home. Sat back in my wooden seat where I accurately predicted "I'm not ready" the night before.

Relieved it was over but disappointed with my performance, I placed a sheet of paper on the desk. I wrote "MY PROBLEMS" at the top, and under that, my prompt for the evening: "What did I do so badly? Why did everything feel so off? Why did the speech fail?"

"You stood in front of 200 people and looked at... a piece of paper, not unlike this one. What the hell were you thinking? You're not fooling anyone by reading a sentence and then looking up at them as you say it out loud. They know you're reading a manuscript, and they know what that means. You are unsure of yourself. You are unsure of your message. You are unprepared. Next: Why did you speak in that odd, low, monotone voice? That sounded like nails on a chalkboard. And it was inauthentic. Next: Why did you open by talking about yourself? Also, you're not particularly funny. No more jokes. And what was the structure of the speech? It had no structure. That, I feel, is probably a pretty big problem."

I believed in my idea, and I wanted to get it across. Of course, I wanted the tangible markers of a successful speech. I wanted action. I wanted the speech to change something in the real world. But my motivations were deeper than that. I wanted to see people "click" and come on board my way of thinking. I wanted to captivate the audience. I wanted to speak with an engaging, impactful voice, drawing the audience in, not repelling them. I wanted them to remember my message and to remember me. I wanted to feel, for just a moment, the thrill of power. But not the petty, forceful power of tyrants and dictators; the justified power – the earned power – of having a good idea and conveying it well; the power of Martin Luther King and John F. Kennedy; a power harnessed in service of a valuable idea, not the personal privilege of the speaker. And I wanted confidence: the quiet strength that comes from knowing your words don't stand in your way, but propel you and the ideas you care about to glorious new mountaintops.

Instead, I stood before the audience, essentially powerless. I spoke for 20 painful minutes – painful for them and for me – and then sat down. I barely made a dent in anyone's consciousness. I generated no excitement. Self-doubt draped its cold embrace over me. Anxiety built a wall between "what I am" and "what I could be."

I had tried so many different solutions. I read countless books on effective communication, asked countless effective communicators for their advice, and consumed countless courses on powerful public speaking. Nothing worked. All the "solutions" that didn't really solve my problem had one thing in common: they treated communication as an abstract art form. They were filled with vague, abstract pieces of advice like "think positive thoughts" and "be yourself." They confused me more than anything else. Instead of illuminating the secrets I had been looking for, they shrouded the elusive but indispensable skill of powerful speaking in uncertainty.

I knew I had to master communication. I knew that the world's most successful people are all great communicators. I knew that effective communication is the bridge between "what I have" and "what I want," or at least an essential part of that bridge. I knew that without effective communication – without the ability to influence, inspire, captivate, and move – I would be all but powerless.

I knew that the person who can speak up but doesn't is no better off than the person who can't speak at all. I heard a wise man say "If you can think and speak and write, you are absolutely deadly. Nothing can get in your way." I heard another wise man say "Speech is power: speech is to persuade, to convert, to compel. It is to bring another out of his bad sense into your good sense." I heard a renowned psychologist say "If you look at people who are remarkably successful across life, there's various reasons. But one of them is that they're unbelievably good at articulating what they're aiming at and strategizing and negotiating and enticing people with a vision forward. Get your words together... that makes you unstoppable. If you are an effective writer and speaker and communicator, you have all the authority and competence that there is."

When I worked in the Massachusetts State House for the Department of Public Safety and Homeland Security, I had the opportunity to speak with countless senators, state representatives, CEOs, and other successful people. In our conversations, however brief, I always asked the same question: "What are the ingredients of your success? What got you where you are?" 100% of them said effective communication. There was not one who said anything else. No matter their field – whether they were entrepreneurs, FBI agents, political leaders, business leaders, or multimillionaire donors – they all pointed to one skill: the ability to convey powerful words in powerful ways. Zero exceptions.

Can you believe it? It still astonishes me.

My problem, and I bet this may be your obstacle as well, was that most of the advice I consumed on this critical skill barely scratched the surface. Sure, it didn't make matters worse, and it certainly offered some improvement, but only in inches when I needed progress in miles. If I stuck with the mainstream public speaking advice, I knew I wouldn't unleash the power of my words. And if I didn't do that, I knew I would always accomplish much less than I could. I knew I would suffocate my own potential. I knew I would feel a rush of crippling anxiety every time I was asked to give a presentation. I knew I would live a life of less fulfillment, less success, less achievement, more frustration, more difficulty, and more anxiety. I knew my words would never become all they could be, which means that I would never become all I could be.

To make matters worse, the mainstream advice – which is not wrong, but simply not deep enough – is everywhere. Almost every article, book, or course published on this subject falls into the mainstream category. And to make matters worse, it's almost impossible to know that until you've spent your hard-earned money and scarce time with the resource. And even then, you might just shrug, and assume that shallow, abstract advice is all there is to the "art" of public speaking. As far as I'm concerned, this is a travesty.

I kept writing. "It felt like there was no real motive; no real impulse to action. Why did they need to act? You didn't tell them. What would happen if they didn't? You didn't tell them that either. Also, you tried too hard to put on a formal façade; you spoke in strange, twisted ways. It didn't sound sophisticated. And your mental game was totally off. You let your mind fill with destructive, doubtful, self-defeating thoughts. And your preparation was totally backward. It did more to set bad habits in stone than it did to set you up for success. And you tried to build suspense at one point but revealed the final point way too early, ruining the effect."

I went on and on until I had a stack of papers filled with problems. "That's no good," I thought. I needed solutions. Everything else I tried failed. But I had one more idea: "I remember reading a great speech. What was it? Oh yeah, that's right: JFK's inaugural address. Let me go pull it up and see why it was so powerful." And that's when everything changed.

I grabbed another sheet of paper. I opened JFK's inaugural address on my laptop. I started reading. Observing. Analyzing.

Reverse-engineering. I started writing down what I saw. Why did it work? Why was it powerful? I was like an archaeologist, digging through his speech for the secrets of powerful communication. I got more and more excited as I kept going. It was late at night, but the shocking and invaluable discoveries I was making gave me a burst of energy. It felt like JFK – one of the most powerful and effective speakers of all time – was coaching me in his rhetorical secrets, showing me how to influence an audience, draw them into my narrative, and find words that get results.

"Oh, so that's how you grab attention."

"Aha! So, if I tell them this, they will see why it matters."

"Fascinating – I can apply this same structure to my speech."

Around 3:00 in the morning, an epiphany hit me like a ton of bricks. That night, a new paradigm was born. A new opportunity emerged for all those who want to unleash the unstoppable power of their words. This new opportunity changed everything for me and eventually, tens of thousands of others. It is now my mission to bring it to millions, so that good people know what they need to know to use their words to achieve their dreams and improve the world.

Want to hear the epiphany?

The mainstream approach: Communication is an art form. It is unlike those dry, boring, "academic" subjects. There are no formulas. There are no patterns. It's all about thinking positive thoughts, faking confidence, and making eye contact. Some people are naturally gifted speakers. For others, the highest skill level they can attain is "not horrible."

The consequences of the mainstream approach: Advice that barely scratches the surface of the power of words. Advice that touches only the tip of the tip of the iceberg. A limited body of knowledge that blinds itself to thousands of hidden, little-known communication strategies that carry immense power; that blinds itself to 95% of what great communication really is. Self-limiting dogmas about who can do what, and how great communicators become great. Half the progress in twice the time, and everything that entails: missed opportunities, unnecessary and preventable frustration and anxiety, and confusion about what to say and how to say it. How do I know? Because I've been there. It's not pretty.

My epiphany, the new Speak for Success paradigm: Communication is as much a science as it is an art. You can study words that changed the world, uncover the hidden secrets of their power, and apply these proven principles to your own message. You can discover precisely what made great communicators great and adopt the same strategies. You can do this without being untrue to yourself or flatly imitating others. In fact, you can do this while being truer to yourself and more original than you ever have been before. Communication is not unpredictable, wishy-washy, or abstract. You can apply predictable processes and principles to reach your goals and get results. You can pick and choose from thousands of little-known speaking strategies, combining your favorite to create a unique communication approach that suits you perfectly. You can effortlessly use the same tactics of the world's most transformational leaders and speakers, and do so automatically, by default, without even thinking about it, as a matter of effortless habit. That's power.

The benefits of the Speak for Success paradigm: Less confusion. More confidence. Less frustration. More clarity. Less anxiety. More courage. You understand the whole iceberg of effective communication. As a result, your words captivate others. You draw them into a persuasive narrative, effortlessly linking your desires and their motives. You know exactly what to say. You know exactly how to say it. You know exactly how to keep your head clear; you are a master of the mental game. Your words can move mountains. Your words are the most powerful tools in your arsenal, and you use them to seize opportunities, move your mission forward, and make the world a better place. Simply put, you speak for success.

Fast forward a few years.

I was sitting in my office at my small wooden desk. My breaths were deep, slow, and steady. My entire being – mind, body, soul – was poised and focused. I set my speech manuscript to the side. I glanced at the clock: 12:01 AM. "Let's go. I'm ready."

I had to speak in front of 200 people the next morning. I had to convince them to put faith in my idea. And I was thrilled, filled with genuine gratitude at the opportunity to do what I love: get up in front of a crowd, think clearly, speak well, and get the job done.

I slept deeply. I dreamt vividly. I saw myself giving the speech. I saw myself victorious, in every sense of the word. I heard applause. I saw their facial expressions. I rose. My head was clear. My mental game was pristine. My mind was an ally, not an obstacle.

"This is going to be fun."

"I'll do my best, and whatever happens, happens."

"I'm so lucky that I get to do this again."

I put on my lucky outfit: the blue suit and the blue-gold watch.

"Remember the principles. They work."

"You developed a great plan last night. It's a winner."

"I can't wait."

The rest went how you would expect. I ate breakfast. Got in my car. Drove. Arrived. Waited. Waited. Waited. Spoke. Succeeded. Walked back to my seat. Waited. Waited. Waited. Got in my car. Drove. Arrived home. Sat back in my wooden seat where I accurately predicted "I'm ready" the night before.

I got my idea across perfectly. My message succeeded: it motivated action and created real-world change. I saw people "click" when I hit the rhetorical peak of my speech. I saw them leaning forward, totally hushed, completely absorbed. I applied the proven principles of engaging and impactful vocal modulation. I knew they would remember me and my message; I engineered my words to be memorable. I felt the thrilling power of giving a great speech. I felt the quiet confidence of knowing that my words carried weight; that they could win hearts, change minds, and help me reach the heights of my potential. I tore off the cold embrace of self-doubt. I defeated communication anxiety and broke down the wall between "what I am" and "what I could be."

Disappointed it was over but pleased with my performance, I placed a sheet of paper on the desk. I wrote "Speak Truth Well" and started planning what would become my business.

To date, we have helped tens of thousands of people gain an unfair advantage in their career, business, and life by unleashing the power of their words. And they experienced the exact same transformation I experienced when they applied the system.

If you tried to master communication before but haven't gotten the results you wanted, it's because of the mainstream approach; an approach that tells you "smiling at the audience" and "making eye contact" is all you need to know to speak well. That's not exactly a malicious lie – they don't know any better – but it is completely incorrect and severely harmful.

If you've been concerned that you won't be able to become a vastly more effective and confident communicator, I want to put those fears to rest. I felt the same way. The people I work with felt the same way. We just needed the right system. One public speaking book written by the director of a popular public speaking forum – I won't name names – wants you to believe that there are "nine public speaking secrets of the world's top minds." Wrong: There are many more than nine. If you feel that anyone who would boil down communication to just nine secrets is either missing something or holding it back, you're right. And the alternative is a much more comprehensive and powerful system. It's a system that gave me and everyone I worked with the transformation we were looking for.

Want to Talk? Email Me:

PANDREIBUSINESS@GMAIL.COM

This is My Personal Email.
I Read Every Message and
Respond in Under 12 Hours.

Visit Our Digital Headquarters:

WWW.SPEAKFORSUCCESSHUB.COM

See All Our Free Resources, Books, Courses, and Services.

THE 15-BOOK SPEAK FOR SUCCESS COLLECTION

confidence, leadership, charisma, influence, public speaking, eloquence, human nature, credibility – it's all here, in a unified collection

MASTER EVERY ASPECT OF COMMUNICATION

THE BESTSELLING SPEAK FOR SUCCESS COLLECTION covers every aspect of communication. Each book in the collection includes diagrams that visualize the essential principles, chapter summaries that remind you of the main ideas, and checklists of the action items in each section, all designed to help you consult the set as a reference.

This series is a cohesive, comprehensive set. After writing the first book, I realized how much information I couldn't fit into it. I wrote the second. After writing the second, the same thing happened. I wrote the third. The pattern continued. As of this writing, there are fifteen books in the collection. After writing each book, I felt called to write another. It is the ultimate communication encyclopedia.

Aside from a small amount of necessary overlap on the basics, each book is a distinct unit that focuses on an entirely new set of principles, strategies, and communication secrets. For example, *Eloquence* reveals the secrets of language that sounds good; *Trust is Power* reveals the secrets of speaking with credibility; *Public Speaking Mastery* reveals a blueprint for delivering speeches.

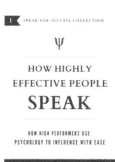

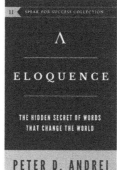

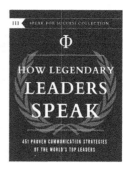

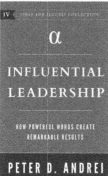

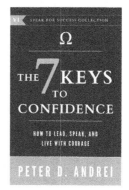

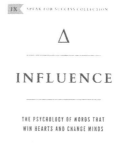

"*The most complete and comprehensive collection of communication wisdom ever compiled.*" – Amazon Customer

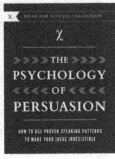
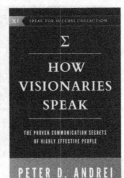
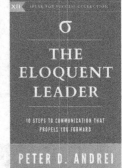

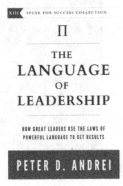
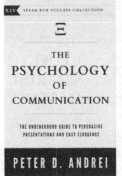
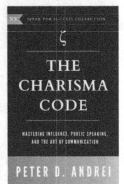

"I love the diagrams and summary checklists. I have all 15 on my shelf, and regularly refer back to them." – *Amazon Customer*

You Can Learn More Here:
www.speakforsuccesshub.com/series

....A Brief Overview.................................

- I wrote *How Highly Effective People Speak* to reveal the hidden patterns in the words of the world's most successful and powerful communicators, so that you can adopt the same tactics and speak with the same impact and influence.
- I wrote *Eloquence* to uncover the formulas of beautiful, moving, captivating, and powerful words, so that you can use these exact same step-by-step structures to quickly make your language electrifying, charismatic, and eloquent.
- I wrote *How Legendary Leaders Speak* to illuminate the little-known five-step communication process the top leaders of the past 500 years all used to spread their message, so that you can use it to empower your ideas and get results.
- I wrote *Influential Leadership* to expose the differences between force and power and to show how great leaders use the secrets of irresistible influence to develop gentle power, so that you can move forward and lead with ease.
- I wrote *Public Speaking Mastery* to shatter the myths and expose the harmful advice about public speaking, and to offer a proven, step-by-step framework for speaking well, so that you can always speak with certainty and confidence.
- I wrote *The 7 Keys to Confidence* to bring to light the ancient 4,000-year-old secrets I used to master the mental game and speak in front of hundreds without a second of self-doubt or anxiety, so that you can feel the same freedom.
- I wrote *Trust is Power* to divulge how popular leaders and career communicators earn our trust, speak with credibility, and use this to rise to new heights of power, so that you can do the same thing to advance your purpose and mission.
- I wrote *Decoding Human Nature* to answer the critical question "what do people want?" and reveal how to use this

knowledge to develop unparalleled influence, so that people adopt your idea, agree with your position, and support you.

- I wrote *Influence* to unearth another little-known five-step process for winning hearts and changing minds, so that you can know with certainty that your message will persuade people, draw support, and motivate enthusiastic action.

- I wrote *The Psychology of Persuasion* to completely and fully unveil everything about the psychology behind "Yes, I love it! What's the next step?" so that you can use easy step-by-step speaking formulas that get people to say exactly that.

- I wrote *How Visionaries Speak* to debunk common lies about effective communication that hold you back and weaken your words, so that you can boldly share your ideas without accidentally sabotaging your own message.

- I wrote *The Eloquent Leader* to disclose the ten steps to communicating with power and persuasion, so that you don't miss any of the steps and fail to connect, captivate, influence, and inspire in a crucial high-stakes moment.

- I wrote *The Language of Leadership* to unpack the unique, hidden-in-plain-sight secrets of how presidents and world-leaders build movements with the laws of powerful language, so that you use them to propel yourself forward.

- I wrote *The Psychology of Communication* to break the news that most presentations succeed or fail in the first thirty seconds and to reveal proven, step-by-step formulas that grab, hold, and direct attention, so that yours succeeds.

- I wrote *The Charisma Code* to shatter the myths and lies about charisma and reveal its nature as a concrete skill you can master with proven strategies, so that people remember you, your message, and how you electrified the room.

- **Learn more: www.speakforsuccesshub.com/series**

III

PRACTICAL TACTICS AND ETHICAL PRINCIPLES

how to easily put complex strategies into action and how to use the power of words to improve the world in an ethical and effective way

MOST COMMUNICATION BOOKS

HAVE YOU READ ANOTHER BOOK ON COMMUNICATION? If you have, let me remind you what you probably learned. And if you haven't, let me briefly spoil 95% of them. "Prepare. Smile. Dress to impress. Keep it simple. Overcome your fears. Speak from the heart. Be authentic. Show them why you care. Speak in terms of their interests. To defeat anxiety, know your stuff. Emotion persuades, not logic. Speak with confidence. Truth sells. And respect is returned."

There you have it. That is most of what you learn in most communication books. None of it is wrong. None of it is misleading. Those ideas are true and valuable. But they are not enough. They are only the absolute basics. And my job is to offer you much more.

Einstein said that "if you can't explain it in a sentence, you don't know it well enough." He also told us to "make it as simple as possible, but no simpler." You, as a communicator, must satisfy both of these maxims, one warning against the dangers of excess complexity, and one warning against the dangers of excess simplicity.

And I, as someone who communicates about communication in my books, courses, and coaching, must do the same.

THE SPEAK FOR SUCCESS SYSTEM

The Speak for Success system makes communication as simple as possible. Other communication paradigms make it even simpler. Naturally, this means our system is more complex. This is an unavoidable consequence of treating communication as a deep and concrete science instead of a shallow and abstract art. If you don't dive into learning communication at all, you miss out. I'm sure you agree with that. But if you don't dive *deep*, you still miss out.

THE FOUR QUADRANTS OF COMMUNICATION

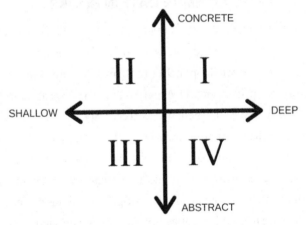

FIGURE VIII: There are four predominant views of communication (whether it takes the form of public speaking, negotiation, writing, or debating is irrelevant). The first view is that communication is concrete and deep. The second view is that communication is concrete and shallow. The third view is that communication is shallow and abstract. The fourth view is that communication is deep and abstract.

WHAT IS COMMUNICATION?

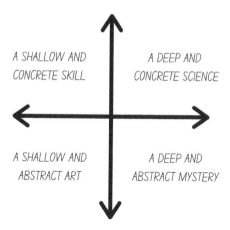

FIGURE VII: The first view treats communication as a science: "There are concrete formulas, rules, principles, and strategies, and they go very deep." The second view treats it as a skill: "Yes, there are concrete formulas, rules, and strategies, but they don't go very deep." The third view treats it as an art: "Rules? Formulas? It's not that complicated. Just smile and think positive thoughts." The fourth view treats it as a mystery: "How are some people such effective communicators? I will never know…"

WHERE WE STAND ON THE QUESTION

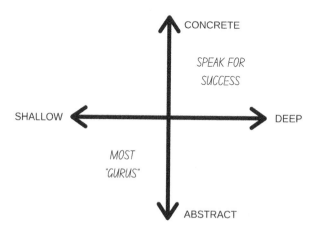

FIGURE VI: Speak for Success takes the view that communication is a deep and concrete science. (And by

"takes the view," I mean "has discovered.") Most other
communication writers, thought-leaders, public speaking
coaches, and individuals and organizations in this niche
treat communication as a shallow and abstract art.

This doesn't mean the Speak for Success system neglects the
basics. It only means it goes far beyond the basics, and that it doesn't
turn simple ideas into 200 pages of filler. It also doesn't mean that
the Speak for Success system is unnecessarily complex. It is as simple
as it can possibly be.

In this book, and in the other books of the Speak for Success
collection, you'll find simple pieces of advice, easy formulas, and
straightforward rules. You'll find theories, strategies, tactics, mental
models, and principles. None of this should pose a challenge. But
you'll also find advanced and complicated strategies. These might.

What is the purpose of the guide on the top of the next page? To
reveal the methods that make advanced strategies easy. When you
use the tactics revealed in this guide, the difficulty of using the
advanced strategies drops dramatically. They empower you to use
complicated and unfamiliar persuasive strategies with ease. If the 15-
book Speak for Success collection is a complete encyclopedia of
communication, to be used like a handbook, then this guide is a
handbook for the handbook.

A SAMPLING OF EASY AND HARD STRATEGIES

Easy and Simple	Hard and Complicated
Use Four-Corner Eye Contact	The Fluency-Magnitude Matrix
Appeal to Their Values	The VPB Triad
Describe the Problem You Solve	The Illusory Truth Effect
Use Open Body Language	Percussive Rhythm
Tell a Quick Story	Alliterative Flow
Appeal to Emotion	Stacking and Layering Structures
Project Your Voice	The Declaratory Cascade
Keep it as Simple as Possible	Alternating Semantic Sentiments

THE PRACTICAL TACTICS

RECOGNIZE THAT, WITH PRACTICE, YOU can use any strategy extemporaneously. Some people can instantly use even the most complex strategies in the Speak for Success collection after reading them just once. They are usually experienced communicators, often with competitive experience. This is not an expectation, but a possibility, and with practice, a probability.

CREATE A COMMUNICATION PLAN. Professional communication often follows a strategic plan. Put these techniques into your plan. Following an effective plan is not harder than following an ineffective one. Marshall your arguments. Marshall your rhetoric. Stack the deck. Know what you know, and how to say it.

DESIGN AN MVP. If you are speaking on short notice, you can create a "minimum viable plan." This can be a few sentences on a notecard jotted down five minutes before speaking. The same principle of formal communication plans applies: While advanced strategies may overburden you if you attempt them in an impromptu setting, putting them into a plan makes them easy.

MASTER YOUR RHETORICAL STACK. Master one difficult strategy. Master another one. Combine them. Master a third. Build out a "rhetorical stack" of ten strategies you can use fluently, in impromptu or extemporaneous communication. Pick strategies that come fluently to you and that complement each other.

PRACTICE THEM TO FLUENCY. I coach a client who approached me and said he wants to master every strategy I ever compiled. That's a lot. As of this writing, we're 90 one-hour sessions in. To warm up for one of our sessions, I gave him a challenge: "Give an impromptu speech on the state of the American economy, and after you stumble, hesitate, or falter four times, I'll cut you off. The challenge is to see how long you can go." He spoke for 20 minutes without a single mistake. After 20 minutes, he brought the impromptu speech to a perfect, persuasive, forceful, and eloquent conclusion. And he naturally and fluently used advanced strategies throughout his impromptu speech. After he closed the speech (which he did because he wanted to get on with the session), I asked him if he thought deeply about the strategies he used. He said no. He used them thoughtlessly. Why? Because he practiced them. You can too. You can practice them on your own. You don't need an audience. You don't need a coach. You don't even need to speak. Practice in your head. Practice ones that resonate with you. Practice with topics you care about.

KNOW TEN TIMES MORE THAN YOU INTEND TO SAY. And know what you do intend to say about ten times more fluently than you need to. This gives your mind room to relax, and frees up cognitive bandwidth to devote to strategy and rhetoric in real-time. Need to speak for five minutes? Be able to speak for 50. Need to read it three times to be able to deliver it smoothly? Read it 30 times.

INCORPORATE THEM IN SLIDES. You can use your slides or visual aids to help you ace complicated strategies. If you can't remember the five steps of a strategy, your slides can still follow them. Good slides aren't harder to use than bad slides.

USE THEM IN WRITTEN COMMUNICATION. You can read your speech. In some situations, this is more appropriate than impromptu or extemporaneous speaking. And if a strategy is difficult to remember in impromptu speaking, you can write it into your speech. And let's not forget about websites, emails, letters, etc.

PICK AND CHOOSE EASY ONES. Use strategies that come naturally and don't overload your mind. Those that do are counterproductive in fast-paced situations.

TAKE SMALL STEPS TO MASTERY. Practice one strategy. Practice it again. Keep going until you master it. Little by little, add to your base of strategies. But never take steps that overwhelm you. Pick a tactic. Practice it. Master it. Repeat.

MEMORIZE AN ENTIRE MESSAGE. Sometimes this is the right move. Is it a high-stakes message? Do you have the time? Do you have the energy? Given the situation, would a memorized delivery beat an impromptu, in-the-moment, spontaneous delivery? If you opt for memorizing, using advanced strategies is easy.

USE ONE AT A TIME. Pick an advanced strategy. Deliver it. Now what? Pick another advanced strategy. Deliver it. Now another. Have you been speaking for a while? Want to bring it to a close? Pick a closing strategy. For some people, using advanced strategies extemporaneously is easy, but only if they focus on one at a time.

MEMORIZE A KEY PHRASE. Deliver your impromptu message as planned, but add a few short, memorized key phrases throughout that include advanced strategies.

CREATE TALKING POINTS. Speak from a list of pre-written bullet-points; big-picture ideas you seek to convey. This is halfway between fully impromptu speaking and using a script. It's not harder to speak from a strategic and persuasively-advanced list of talking points than it is to speak from a persuasively weak list. You can either memorize your talking points, or have them in front of you as a guide.

TREAT IT LIKE A SCIENCE. At some point, you struggled with a skill that you now perform effortlessly. You mastered it. It's a habit. You do it easily, fluently, and thoughtlessly. You can do it while you daydream. Communication is the same. These tactics, methods, and strategies are not supposed to be stuck in the back of your mind as you speak. They are supposed to be ingrained in your habits.

RELY ON FLOW. In fast-paced and high-stakes situations, you usually don't plan every word, sentence, and idea consciously and deliberately. Rather, you let your subconscious mind take over. You speak from a flow state. In flow, you may flawlessly execute strategies that would have overwhelmed your conscious mind.

LISTEN TO THE PROMPTS. You read a strategy and found it difficult to use extemporaneously. But as you speak, your subconscious mind gives you a prompt:

"this strategy would work great here." Your subconscious mind saw the opportunity and surfaced the prompt. You execute it, and you do so fluently and effortlessly.

FOLLOW THE FIVE-STEP CYCLE. First, find truth. Research. Prepare. Learn. Second, define your message. Figure out what you believe about what you learned. Third, polish your message with rhetorical strategies, without distorting the precision with which it conveys the truth. Fourth, practice the polished ideas. Fifth, deliver them. The endeavor of finding truth comes before the rhetorical endeavor. First, find the right message. Then, find the best way to convey it.

CREATE YOUR OWN STRATEGY. As you learn new theories, mental models, and principles of psychology and communication, you may think of a new strategy built around the theories, models, and principles. Practice it, test it, and codify it.

STACK GOOD HABITS. An effective communicator is the product of his habits. If you want to be an effective communicator, stack good communication habits (and break bad ones). This is a gradual process. It doesn't happen overnight.

DON'T TRY TO USE THEM. Don't force it. If a strategy seems too difficult, don't try to use it. You might find yourself using it anyway when the time is right.

KNOW ONLY ONE. If you master one compelling communication strategy, like one of the many powerful three-part structures that map out a persuasive speech, that can often be enough to drastically and dramatically improve your impact.

REMEMBER THE SHORTCOMING OF MODELS. All models are wrong, but some are useful. Many of these complex strategies and theories are models. They represent reality, but they are not reality. They help you navigate the territory, but they are not the territory. They are a map, to be used if it helps you navigate, and to be discarded the moment it prevents you from navigating.

DON'T LET THEM INHIBIT YOU. Language flows from thought. You've got to have something to say. And *then* you make it as compelling as possible. And *then* you shape it into something poised and precise; persuasive and powerful; compelling and convincing. Meaning and message come first. Rhetoric comes second. Don't take all this discussion of "advanced communication strategies," "complex communication tactics," and "the deep and concrete science of communication" to suggest that the basics don't matter. They do. Tell the truth as precisely and boldly as you can. Know your subject-matter like the back of your hand. Clear your mind and focus on precisely articulating exactly what you believe to be true. Be authentic. The advanced strategies are not supposed to stand between you and your audience. They are not supposed to stand between you and your authentic and spontaneous self – they are supposed to be integrated with it. They are not an end in themselves, but a means to the end of persuading the maximum number of people to adopt truth. Trust your instinct. Trust your intuition. It won't fail you.

MASTERING ONE COMMUNICATION SKILL

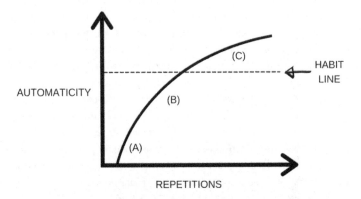

FIGURE V: Automaticity is the extent to which you do something automatically, without thinking about it. At the start of building a communication habit, it has low automaticity. You need to think about it consciously (A). After more repetitions, it gets easier and more automatic (B). Eventually, the behavior becomes more automatic than deliberate. At this point, it becomes a habit (C).

MASTERING COMMUNICATION

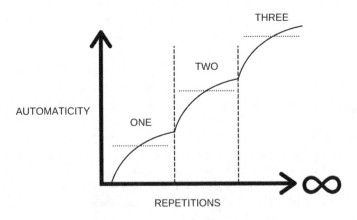

FIGURE IV: Layer good communication habits on top of each other. Go through the learning curve over and over again. When you master the first good habit, jump to the second. This pattern will take you to mastery.

THE FOUR LEVELS OF KNOWING

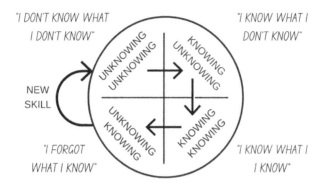

FIGURE III: First, you don't know you don't know it. Then, you discover it and know you don't know it. Then, you practice it and know you know it. Then, it becomes a habit. You forget you know it. It's ingrained in your habits.

REVISITING THE LEARNING CURVE

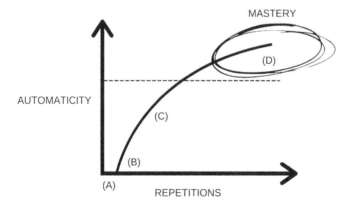

FIGURE II: Note the stages of knowing on the learning curve: unknowing unknowing (A), knowing unknowing (B), knowing knowing (C), unknowing knowing (D).

WHAT'S REALLY HAPPENING?

Have you ever thought deeply about what happens when you communicate? Let's run through the mile-high view.

At some point in your life, you bumped into an experience. You observed. You learned. The experience changed you. Your neural networks connected in new ways. New rivers of neurons began to flow through them.

The experience etched a pattern into your neurobiology representing information about the moral landscape of the universe; a map of *where we are, where we should go, and how we should make the journey.* This is meaning. This is your message.

Now, you take the floor before a crowd. Whether you realize it or not, you want to copy the neural pattern from your mind to their minds. You want to show them where we are, where we should go, and how we should make the journey.

So, you speak. You gesture. You intone. Your words convey meaning. Your body language conveys meaning. Your voice conveys meaning. You flood them with a thousand different inputs, some as subtle as the contraction of a single facial muscle, some as obvious as your opening line. Your character, your intentions, and your goals seep into your speech. Everyone can see them. Everyone can see you.

Let's step into the mind of one of your audience members. Based on all of this, based on a thousand different inputs, based on complex interactions between their conscious and nonconscious minds, the ghost in the machine steps in, and by a dint of free will, acts as the final arbiter and makes a choice. A mind is changed. You changed it. And changing it changed you. You became more confident, more articulate, and deeper; more capable, more impactful, and stronger.

Communication is connection. One mind, with a consciousness at its base, seeks to use ink or pixels or airwaves to connect to another. Through this connection, it seeks to copy neural patterns about the present, the future, and the moral landscape. Whatever your message is, the underlying connection is identical. How could it not be?

IS IT ETHICAL?

By "it," I mean deliberately using language to get someone to do or think something. Let's call this rhetoric. We could just as well call it persuasion, influence, communication, or even leadership itself.

The answer is yes. The answer is no. Rhetoric is a helping hand. It is an iron fist. It is Martin Luther King's dream. It is Stalin's nightmare. It is the "shining city on the hill." It is the iron curtain. It is "the pursuit of happiness." It is the trail of tears. It is "liberty, equality, and brotherhood." It is the reign of terror. Rhetoric is a tool. It is neither good nor evil. It is a reflection of our nature.

Rhetoric can motivate love, peace, charity, strength, patience, progress, prosperity, common sense, common purpose, courage, hope, generosity, and unity. It can also sow the seeds of division, fan the flames of tribalism, and beat back the better angels of our nature.

Rhetoric is the best of us and the worst of us. It is as good as you are. It is as evil as you are. It is as peace-loving as you are. It is as hate-mongering as you are. And I know what you are. I know my readers are generous, hardworking people who want to build a better future for themselves, for their families, and for all humankind. I know that if you have these tools in your hands, you will use them to achieve a moral mission. That's why putting them in your hands is my mission.

Joseph Chatfield said "[rhetoric] is the power to talk people out of their sober and natural opinions." I agree. But it is also the power to talk people out of their wrong and harmful opinions. And if you're using rhetoric to talk people out of their sober opinions, the problem isn't rhetoric, it's you.

In the *Institutes of Rhetoric*, Roman rhetorician Quintilian wrote the following: "The orator then, whom I am concerned to form, shall be the orator as defined by Marcus Cato, a good man, skilled in speaking. But above all he must possess the quality which Cato places first and which is in the very nature of things the greatest and most important, that is, he must be a good man. This is essential not merely on account of the fact that, if the powers of eloquence serve only to lend arms to crime, there can be nothing more pernicious than eloquence to public and private welfare alike, while I myself, who have labored to the best of my ability to contribute something of the value to oratory, shall have rendered the worst of services to mankind, if I forge these weapons not for a soldier, but for a robber."

Saint Augustine, who was trained in the classical schools of rhetoric in the 3rd century, summed it up well: "Rhetoric, after all, being the art of persuading people to accept something, whether it is true or false, would anyone dare to maintain that truth should stand there without any weapons in the hands of its defenders against falsehood; that those speakers, that is to say, who are trying to convince their hearers of what is untrue, should know how to get them on their side, to gain their attention and have them eating out of their hands by their opening remarks, while these who are defending the truth should not? That those should utter their lies briefly, clearly, plausibly, and these should state their truths in a manner too boring to listen to, too obscure to understand, and finally too repellent to believe? That those should attack the truth with specious arguments, and assert falsehoods, while these should be incapable of either defending the truth or refuting falsehood? That those, to move and force the minds of their hearers into error, should be able by their style to terrify them, move them to tears, make them laugh, give them rousing encouragement, while these on behalf of truth stumble along slow, cold and half asleep?"

THE ETHICS OF PERSUASION

REFER BACK TO THIS ETHICAL GUIDE as needed. I created this in a spirit of humility, for my benefit as much as for the benefit of my readers. And you don't have to choose between efficacy and ethics. When I followed these principles, my words became more ethical *and* more powerful.

FOLLOW THESE TWELVE RULES. Do not use false, fabricated, misrepresented, distorted, or irrelevant evidence to support claims. Do not intentionally use specious, unsupported, or illogical reasoning. Do not represent yourself as informed or as an "expert" on a subject when you are not. Do not use irrelevant appeals to divert attention from the issue at hand. Do not cause intense but unreflective emotional reactions. Do not link your idea to emotion-laden values, motives, or goals to which it is not related. Do not hide your real purpose or self-interest, the group you represent, or your position as an advocate of a viewpoint. Do not distort, hide, or misrepresent the number, scope, or intensity of bad effects. Do not use emotional appeals that lack a basis of evidence or reasoning or that would fail if the audience examined the subject themselves. Do not oversimplify complex, gradation-laden situations into simplistic two-valued, either/or, polar views or choices. Do not pretend certainty where tentativeness and degrees of probability would be more accurate. Do not advocate something you do not believe (Johannesen et al., 2021).

APPLY THIS GOLDEN HEURISTIC. In a 500,000-word book, you might be able to tell your audience everything you know about a subject. In a five-minute persuasive speech, you can only select a small sampling of your knowledge. Would learning your entire body of knowledge result in a significantly different reaction than hearing the small sampling you selected? If the answer is yes, that's a problem.

SWING WITH THE GOOD EDGE. Rhetoric is a double-edged sword. It can express good ideas well. It can also express bad ideas well. Rhetoric makes ideas attractive; tempting; credible; persuasive. Don't use it to turn weakly-worded lies into well-worded lies. Use it to turn weakly-worded truths into well-worded truths.

TREAT TRUTH AS THE HIGHEST GOOD. Use any persuasive strategy, unless using it in your circumstances would distort the truth. The strategies should not come between you and truth, or compromise your honesty and authenticity.

AVOID THE SPIRIT OF DECEIT. Wrong statements are incorrect statements you genuinely believe. Lies are statements you know are wrong but convey anyway. Deceitful statements are not literally wrong, but you convey them with the intent to mislead, obscure, hide, or manipulate. Hiding relevant information is not literally lying (saying you conveyed all the information would be). Cherry-picking facts is not literally lying (saying there are no other facts would be). Using clever innuendo to twist reality without making any concrete claims is not literally lying (knowingly making a false accusation would be). And yet, these are all examples of deceit.

ONLY USE STRATEGIES IF THEY ARE ACCURATE. Motivate unified thinking. Inspire loving thinking. These strategies sound good. Use the victim-perpetrator-benevolence structure. Paint a common enemy. Appeal to tribal psychology. These strategies sound bad. But when reality lines up with the strategies that sound bad, they become good. They are only bad when they are inaccurate or move people down a bad path. *But the same is true for the ones that sound good.* Should Winston Churchill have motivated unified thinking? Not toward his enemy. Should he have avoided appealing to tribal psychology to strengthen the Allied war effort? Should he have avoided painting a common enemy? Should he have avoided portraying the victimization of true victims and the perpetration of a true perpetrator? Should he have avoided calling people to act as the benevolent force for good, protecting the victim and beating back the perpetrator? Don't use the victim-perpetrator-benevolence structure if there aren't clear victims and perpetrators. This is demagoguery. Painting false victims disempowers them. But if there are true victims and perpetrators, stand up for the victims and stand against the perpetrators, calling others to join you as a benevolent force for justice. Don't motivate unified thinking when standing against evil. Don't hold back from portraying a common enemy when there is one. Some strategies might sound morally suspect. Some might sound inherently good. But it depends on the situation. Every time I say "do X to achieve Y," remember the condition: "if it is accurate and moves people up a good path."

APPLY THE TARES TEST: truthfulness of message, authenticity of persuader, respect for audience, equity of persuasive appeal, and social impact (TARES).

REMEMBER THE THREE-PART VENN DIAGRAM: words that are authentic, effective, and true. Donald Miller once said "I'm the kind of person who wants to present my most honest, authentic self to the world, so I hide backstage and rehearse honest and authentic lines until the curtain opens." There's nothing dishonest or inauthentic about choosing your words carefully and making them more effective, as long as they remain just as true. Rhetoric takes a messy marble brick of truth and sculpts it into a poised, precise, and perfect statue. It takes weak truths and makes them strong. Unfortunately, it can do the same for weak lies. But preparing, strategizing, and sculpting is not inauthentic. Unskillfulness is no more authentic than skillfulness. Unpreparedness is no more authentic than preparedness.

APPLY FITZPATRICK AND GAUTHIER'S THREE-QUESTION ANALYSIS. For what purpose is persuasion being employed? Toward what choices and with what consequences for individual lives is it being used? Does the persuasion contribute to or interfere with the audience's decision-making process (Lumen, 2016)?

STRENGTHEN THE TRUTH. Rhetoric makes words strong. Use it to turn truths strong, not falsities strong. There are four categories of language: weak and wrong, strong and wrong, weak and true, strong and true. Turn weak and true language into strong and true language. Don't turn weak and wrong language into strong and wrong language, weak and true language into strong and wrong language, or strong and true language into weak and true language. Research. Question your assumptions. Strive for truth. Ensure your logic is impeccable. Defuse your biases.

START WITH FINDING TRUTH. The rhetorical endeavor starts with becoming as knowledgeable on your subject as possible and developing an impeccable logical argument. The more research you do, the more rhetoric you earn the right to use.

PUT TRUTH BEFORE STYLE. Rhetorical skill does not make you correct. Truth doesn't care about your rhetoric. If your rhetoric is brilliant, but you realize your arguments are simplistic, flawed, or biased, change course. Let logic lead style. Don't sacrifice logic to style. Don't express bad ideas well. Distinguish effective speaking from effective rational argument. Achieve both, but put reason and logic first.

AVOID THE POPULARITY VORTEX. As Plato suggested, avoid "giving the citizens what they want [in speech] with no thought to whether they will be better or worse as a result of what you are saying." Ignore the temptation to gain positive reinforcement and instant gratification from the audience with no merit to your message. Rhetoric is unethical if used solely to appeal rather than to help the world.

CONSIDER THE CONSEQUENCES. If you succeed to persuade people, will the world become better or worse? Will your audience benefit? Will you benefit? Moreover, is it the best action they could take? Or would an alternative help more? Is it an objectively worthwhile investment? Is it the best solution? Are you giving them all the facts they need to determine this on their own?

CONSIDER SECOND- AND THIRD-ORDER IMPACTS. Consider not only immediate consequences, but consequences across time. Consider the impact of the action you seek to persuade, as well as the tools you use to persuade it. Maybe the action is objectively positive, but in motivating the action, you resorted to instilling beliefs that will cause damage over time. Consider their long-term impact as well.

KNOW THAT BAD ACTORS ARE PLAYING THE SAME GAME. Bad actors already know how to be persuasive and how to spread their lies. They already know the tools. And many lies are more tempting than truth and easier to believe by their very nature. Truth waits for us to find it at the bottom of a muddy well. Truth is complicated, and complexity is harder to convey with impact. Use these tools to give truth a fighting chance in an arena where bad actors have a natural advantage. Use your knowledge to counter and defuse these tools when people misuse them.

APPLY THE FIVE ETHICAL APPROACHES: seek the greatest good for the greatest number (utilitarian); protect the rights of those affected and treat people not as means but as ends (rights); treat equals equally and nonequals fairly (justice); set the good of humanity as the basis of your moral reasoning (common good); act consistently with the ideals that lead to your self-actualization and the highest potential of your character (virtue). Say and do what is right, not what is expedient, and be willing to suffer the consequences of doing so. Don't place self-gratification, acquisitiveness, social status, and power over the common good of all humanity.

APPLY THE FOUR ETHICAL DECISION-MAKING CRITERIA: respect for individual rights to make choices, hold views, and act based on personal beliefs and values (autonomy); the maximization of benefits and the minimization of harms, acting for the benefit of others, helping others further their legitimate interests; taking action to prevent or remove possible harms (beneficence); acting in ways that cause no harm, avoid the risk of harm, and assuring benefits outweigh costs (non-maleficence); treating others according to a defensible standard (justice).

USE ILLOGICAL PROCESSES TO GET ETHICAL RESULTS. Using flawed thinking processes to get good outcomes is not unethical. Someone who disagrees should stop speaking with conviction, clarity, authority, and effective paralanguage. All are irrelevant to the truth of their words, but impact the final judgment of the audience. You must use logic and evidence to figure out the truth. But this doesn't mean logic and evidence will persuade others. Humans have two broad categories of cognitive functions: system one is intuitive, emotional, fast, heuristic-driven, and generally illogical; system two is rational, deliberate, evidence-driven, and generally logical. The best-case scenario is to get people to believe right things for right reasons (through system two). The next best case is to get people to believe right things for wrong reasons (through system one). Both are far better than letting people believe wrong things for wrong reasons. If you don't use those processes, they still function, but lead people astray. You can reverse-engineer them. If you know the truth, have an abundance of reasons to be confident you know the truth, and can predict the disasters that will occur if people don't believe the truth, don't you have a responsibility to be as effective as possible in bringing people to the truth? Logic and evidence are essential, of course. They will persuade many. They should have persuaded you. But people can't always follow a long chain of reasoning or a complicated argument. Persuade by eloquence what you learned by reason.

HELP YOUR SELF-INTEREST. (But not at the expense of your audience or without their knowledge). Ethics calls for improving the world, and you are a part of the world – the one you control most. Improving yourself is a service to others.

APPLY THE WINDOWPANE STANDARD. In Aristotle's view, rhetoric reveals how to persuade and how to defeat manipulative persuaders. Thus, top students of rhetoric would be master speakers, trained to anticipate and disarm the rhetorical tactics of their adversaries. According to this tradition, language is only useful to the extent that it does not distort reality, and good writing functions as a "windowpane," helping people peer through the wall of ignorance and view reality. You might think this precludes persuasion. You might think this calls for dry academic language. But what good is a windowpane if nobody cares to look through it? What good is a windowpane to reality if, on the other wall, a stained-glass window distorts reality but draws people to it? The best windowpane reveals as much of reality as possible while drawing as many people to it as possible.

RUN THROUGH THESE INTROSPECTIVE QUESTIONS. Are the means truly unethical or merely distasteful, unpopular, or unwise? Is the end truly good, or does it simply appear good because we desire it? Is it probable that bad means will achieve the good end? Is the same good achievable using more ethical means if we are creative, patient, and skillful? Is the good end clearly and overwhelmingly better than any bad effects of the means used to attain it? Will the use of unethical means to achieve a good end withstand public scrutiny? Could the use of unethical means be justified to those most affected and those most impartial? Can I specify my ethical criteria or standards? What is the grounding of the ethical judgment? Can I justify the reasonableness and relevancy of these standards for this case? Why are these the best criteria? Why do they take priority? How does the communication succeed or fail by these standards? What judgment is justified in this case about the degree of ethicality? Is it a narrowly focused one rather than a broad and generalized one? To whom is ethical responsibility owed – to which individuals, groups, organizations, or professions? In what ways and to what extent? Which take precedence? What is my responsibility to myself and society? How do I feel about myself after this choice? Can I continue to "live with myself?" Would I want my family to know of this choice? Does the choice reflect my ethical character? To what degree is it "out of character?" If called upon in public to justify the ethics of my communication, how adequately could I do so? What generally accepted reasons could I offer? Are there precedents which can guide me? Are there aspects of this case that set it apart from others? How thoroughly have alternatives been explored before settling on this choice? Is it less ethical than some of the workable alternatives? If the goal requires unethical communication, can I abandon the goal (Johannesen et al., 2007)?

VIEW YOURSELF AS A GUIDE. Stories have a hero, a villain who stands in his way, and a guide who helps the hero fulfill his mission. If you speak ineffectively, you are a nonfactor. If you speak deceitfully, you become the villain. But if you convey truth effectively, you become the guide in your audience's story, who leads them, teaches them, inspires them, and helps them overcome adversity and win. Use your words to put people on the best possible path. And if you hide an ugly truth, ask yourself this: "If I found out that *my* guide omitted this, how would I react?"

APPLY THE PUZZLE ANALOGY. Think of rhetoric as a piece in the puzzle of reality. Only use a rhetorical approach if it fits with the most logical, rational, and evidence-based view of reality. If it doesn't, it's the wrong puzzle piece. Try another.

KNOW THAT THE TRUTH WILL OUT. The truth can either come out in your words, or you can deceive people. You can convince them to live in a fantasy. And that might work. Until. Until truth breaks down the door and storms the building. Until the facade comes crashing down and chaos makes its entry. Slay the dragon in its lair before it comes to your village. Invite truth in through the front door before truth burns the building down. Truth wins in the end, either because a good person spreads, defends, and fights for it, or because untruth reveals itself as such by its consequences, and does so in brutal and painful fashion, hurting innocents and perpetrators alike. Trust and reputation take years to create and seconds to destroy.

MAXIMIZE THE TWO HIERARCHIES OF SUCCESS: honesty *and* effectiveness. You could say "Um, well, uh, I think that um, what we should… should uh… do, is that, well… let me think… er, I think if we are more, you know… fluid, we'll be better at… producing, I mean, progressing, and producing, and just more generally, you know, getting better results, but… I guess my point is, like, that, that if we are more fluid and do things more better, we will get better results than with a bureaucracy and, you know how it is, a silo-based structure, right? I mean… you know what I mean." Or, you could say "Bravery beats bureaucracy, courage beats the status quo, and innovation beats stagnation." Is one of those statements truer? No. Is one of them more effective? Is one of them more likely to get positive action that instantiates the truth into the world? Yes. Language is not reality. It provides signposts to reality. Two different signposts can point at the same truth – they can be equally and maximally true – and yet one can be much more effective. One gets people to follow the road. One doesn't. Maximize honesty. Then, insofar as it doesn't sacrifice honesty, maximize effectiveness. Speak truth. And speak it well.

KNOW THAT DECEPTION SINKS THE SHIP. Deception prevents perception. If someone deceives everyone onboard a ship, blinding them in a sense, they may get away with self-serving behavior. But eventually, they get hurt by the fate they designed. The ship sinks. How could it not? The waters are hazardous. If the crew is operating with distorted perceptions, they fail to see the impending dangers in the deep. So it is with teams, organizations, and entire societies.

APPLY THE WISDOM OF THIS QUOTE. Mary Beard, an American historian, author, and activist, captured the essence of ethical rhetoric well: "What politicians do is they never get the rhetoric wrong, and the price they pay is they don't speak the truth as they see it. Now, I will speak truth as I see it, and sometimes I don't get the rhetoric right. I think that's a fair trade-off." It's more than fair. It's necessary.

REMEMBER YOUR RESPONSIBILITY TO SOCIETY. Be a guardian of the truth. Speak out against wrongdoing, and do it well. The solution to evil speech is not less speech, but more (good) speech. Create order with your words, not chaos. Our civilization depends on it. Match the truth, honesty, and vulnerable transparency of your words against the irreducible complexity of the universe. And in this complex universe, remember the omnipresence of nuance, and the dangers of simplistic ideologies. (Inconveniently, simplistic ideologies are persuasive, while nuanced truths are difficult to convey. This is why good people need to be verbally skilled; to pull the extra weight of conveying a realistic worldview). Don't commit your whole mind to an isolated fragment of truth, lacking context, lacking nuance. Be precise in your speech, to ensure you are saying what you mean to say. Memorize the logical fallacies, the cognitive biases, and the rules of logic and correct thinking. (Conveniently, many rhetorical devices are also reasoning devices that focus your inquiry and help you explicate truth). But don't demonize those with good intentions and bad ideas. If they are forthcoming and honest, they are not your enemy. Rather, the two of you are on a shared mission to find the truth, partaking in a shared commitment to reason and dialogue. The malevolent enemy doesn't care about the truth. And in this complex world, remember Voltaire's warning to "cherish those who seek the truth but beware of those who find it," and Aristotle's startling observation that "the least deviation from truth [at the start] is multiplied a thousandfold." Be cautious in determining what to say with conviction. Good speaking is not a substitute for good thinking. The danger zone is being confidently incorrect. What hurts us most is what we know that just isn't so. Remember these tenets and your responsibility, and rhetoric becomes the irreplaceable aid of the good person doing good things in difficult times; the sword of the warrior of the light.

KNOW THAT DECEPTION IS ITS OWN PUNISHMENT. Knowingly uttering a falsehood is a spoken lie of commission. Having something to say but not saying it is a spoken lie of omission. Knowingly behaving inauthentically is an acted-out lie of commission. Knowingly omitting authentic behavior is an acted-out lie of omission. All these deceptions weaken your being. All these deceptions corrupt your own mind, turning your greatest asset into an ever-present companion you can no longer trust. Your conscience operates somewhat autonomously, and it will call you out (unless your repeated neglect desensitizes it). You have a conscious conscience which speaks clearly, and an unconscious conscience, which communicates more subtly. A friend of mine asked: "Why do we feel relieved when we speak truth? Why are we drawn toward it, even if it is not pleasant? Do our brains have something that makes this happen?" Yes, they do: our consciences, our inner lights, our inner north stars. And we feel relieved because living with the knowledge of our own deceit is often an unbearable burden. You live your life before an audience of one: yourself. You cannot escape the observation of your own awareness; you can't hide from yourself. Everywhere you go, there you are. Everything you do, there you are. Some of the greatest heights of wellbeing come from performing well in this one-man theater, and signaling virtue to yourself; being someone you are proud to be (and grateful to observe). Every time you lie, you tell your subconscious mind that your character is too weak to contend with the truth. And this shapes your character accordingly. It becomes true. And then what? Lying carries its own punishment, even if the only person who catches the liar is the liar himself.

BE A MONSTER (THEN LEARN TO CONTROL IT). There is nothing moral about weakness and harmlessness. The world is difficult. There are threats to confront, oppressors to resist, and tyrants to rebuff. (Peterson, 2018). There are psychopaths, sociopaths, and Machiavellian actors with no love for the common good. There is genuine malevolence. If you are incapable of being an effective deceiver, then you are incapable of being an effective advocate for truth: it is the same weapon, pointed in different directions. If you cannot use it in both directions, can you use it at all? Become a monster, become dangerous, and become capable of convincing people to believe in a lie… and then use this ability to convince them to believe in the truth. The capacity for harm is also the capacity for harming harmful entities; that is to say, defending innocent ones. If you can't hurt anyone, you can't help anyone when they need someone to stand up for them. Words are truly weapons, and the most powerful weapons in the world at that. The ability to use them, for good *or* for bad, is the prerequisite to using them for good. There is an archetype in our cultural narratives: the well-intentioned but harmless protagonist who gets roundly defeated by the villain, until he develops his monstrous edge and integrates it, at which point he becomes the triumphant hero. Along similar lines, I watched a film about an existential threat to humanity, in which the protagonist sought to convey the threat to a skeptical public, but failed miserably because he lacked the rhetorical skill to do so. The result? The world ended. Everyone died. The protagonist was of no use to anyone. And this almost became a true story. A historical study showed that in the Cuban Missile Crisis, the arguments that won out in the United States mastermind group were not the best, but those argued with the most conviction. Those with the best arguments lacked the skill to match. The world (could have) ended. The moral? Speak truth… well.

MASTERING COMMUNICATION, ONE SKILL AT A TIME

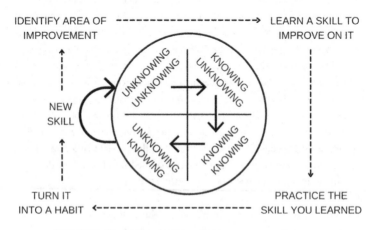

FIGURE I: The proven path to mastery.

language

....

noun

> a system of communication used by a particular country or community

leadership

....

noun

> the action of leading a group of people or an organization

leading

....

adjective

> providing direction or guidance

CONTENTS

WHAT IS LEADERSHIP? 69

DURING WAR: 89

DURING STAGNATION: 231

BEFORE YOU GO…

Rhetoric, Motivated by Love, Guided by Reason, and Aimed at Truth, Is a Powerful Force for the Greatest Good.

POLITICAL DISCLAIMER

Throughout this book, and throughout all my books, I draw examples of communication strategies from the political world. I quote from the speeches of many of America's great leaders, like JFK and MLK, as well as from more recent political figures of both major parties. Political communication is ideal for illustrating the concepts revealed in the books. It is the best source of examples of words that work that I have ever found. I don't use anything out of the political mainstream. And it is by extensively studying the inaugural addresses of United States Presidents and the great speeches of history that I have discovered many of the speaking strategies I share with you.

My using the words of any particular figure to illustrate a principle of communication is not necessarily an endorsement of the figure or their message. Separate the speaker from the strategy. After all, the strategy is the only reason the speaker made an appearance in the book at all. Would you rather have a weak example of a strategy you want to learn from a speaker you love, or a perfect example of the strategy from a speaker you detest?

For a time, I didn't think a disclaimer like this was necessary. I thought people would do this on their own. I thought that if people read an example of a strategy drawn from the words of a political figure they disagreed with, they would appreciate the value of the example as an instructive tool and set aside their negative feelings about the speaker. "Yes, I don't agree with this speaker or the message, but I can clearly see the strategy in this example and I now have a better understanding of how it works and how to execute it." Indeed, I suspect 95% of my readers do just that. You probably will, too. But if you are part of the 5% who aren't up for it, don't say I didn't warn you, and please don't leave a negative review because you think I endorse this person or that person. I don't, as this is strictly a book about communication.

THE

LANGUAGE

OF

LEADERSHIP

HOW GREAT LEADERS USE THE LAWS OF POWERFUL LANGUAGE TO GET RESULTS

SPEAK FOR SUCCESS COLLECTION BOOK

XIII

THE LANGUAGE OF LEADERSHIP CHAPTER

I

WHAT IS LEADERSHIP?

The Best Answer to the Most Important Question

LOOK AROUND YOU

L OOK AROUND YOU. PICK ANY man-made object in your field of vision. Look within you. Pick any idea in your mind. Go to the top of the Empire State Building, and gaze upon the skyline of New York City unfolding below you.

Every object around you, every idea in your heart and mind, and every building in that majestic skyline is the product of the single most powerful force known to man. And what is this unstoppable force? You already know. You just haven't realized it yet.

I discovered it in a dusty old book at the age of eleven, sitting on a pier in Maine (my reading spot, where I still return two decades later). Every single good thing in my life that I intentionally brought into existence was the product of this single secret force.

I'll tell you exactly what it is. But first, let me tell you some more secrets about this little-known force. It cannot be taken away from you. It is entirely within your control. You have used it before. You haven't realized when. Almost every single self-improvement book alludes to it. Even the authors of these books don't realize when they invoke this force. Every single major religious text implies it on nearly every page. Few people find it in the subtext of these holy books. The world often conspires against this force, though nobody can strip it from you but yourself, through neglect of its use. Every single possible goal you seek is attainable through this secret force. And no, you cannot break natural or human law. This applies only in the realm of reasonable reality.

Want to build a business that feeds your family? Want to build an innovation that makes you a millionaire? Want to build a non-profit that changes lives around the world? These exist within the realm of possible, in fact, likely reality, once you harness this force.

Or, to start smaller: Want to advance your career? Want to realize your short-term ambitions? Want to achieve more power over the circumstances of your life? These exist within the realm of inevitable reality once you harness this force.

This force is the only way. But worry not: it is entirely within your control, it is worldly, and it is not as mysterious as I make it out to be. In fact, it is extremely obvious.

So, what is this magical force? There's nothing magical about it at all. It is of this world, and it acts in purely physical, tangible ways. Here it is: controlled human attention, centered on a definite purpose, backed by intentional action, supported by correct thinking, and empowered by a deeper motive.

The book I was reading at eleven that taught me this secret? *Think and Grow Rich*, by Napoleon Hill. Now, you're reading a leadership book, right? So, what does this have to do with leadership? Everything. And here's why: all legendary leaders use this secret force not only within themselves, but within the hearts, minds, and souls of their followers. Napoleon Hill called it the mastermind principle.

And this mastermind principle is the secret of all the leaders who have changed the world, changed the lives of their followers, or converted an inevitable failure into an incredible success.

Think about it: effective leadership is simply channeling the controlled attention of those in your charge, centering it on a definite purpose, backing it by their intentional action, helping them think correctly, and giving them a deeper motive that empowers the entire process.

Weak leaders don't understand this. Average leaders intellectually agree, but don't understand the mechanism for manifesting this. The world's legendary leaders understand the gravity of this fundamental truth and have mastered the mechanism for manifesting it. What do you want to be? Weak, average, or legendary?

This is what will make you the best possible leader you can be: the mechanism for manifesting this force within the hearts, minds, and souls of those in your charge. So, what's the mechanism? Communication.

The leaders who have changed the world have done so by mastering what I call the communication of leadership. Why the fancy name? Because nobody can be a true leader without it.

In other words: every single legendary leader, from Steve Jobs to Bill Gates, to Franklin Delano Roosevelt, to Nelson Mandela, to Mahatma Gandhi, has used the communication of leadership to (1) control the attention of their followers, (2) center the attention of their followers on a definite purpose, (3) back this attention by intentional action, (4) support the action with correct thinking, and (5) empower this entire process with a deep motive.

As we proceed in message-hacking, we will see the steps of this process shine in each message we analyze. While we won't necessarily break down the speeches into the five-step framework, instead focusing on the most impactful strategies in a passage in isolation, you will plainly see the proven process in action.

THE FIVE-STEP PROCESS OF LEGENDARY LEADERS

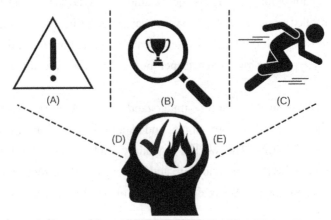

FIGURE 1: First, grab attention (A). Then, direct it to a definite purpose (B). Then, back it with intentional action

(C). Back this entire process with correct thinking (D) and a powerful motive (E).

Through the communication of leadership, they have manifested the single most powerful force known to man on a massive scale, and have achieved whatever they could conceive because of it.

And what does it mean for us that the immortal words of these legendary leaders live on today, and are instantly accessible through Google (which is yet another product of this force being channeled by the communication of leadership on a mass scale)?

This is what it means: that we can pick apart the hidden, little-known, secret strategies that define the communication of leadership, with an in-depth analysis of the world's most legendary pieces of this elevated, surpassing brand of communication. (I call this process message-hacking).

In other words: we can completely unleash the power of the communication of leadership (the same power that brought the United States into existence, defeated Nazism, and built virtually every successful business) and make it accessible to you.

Let me put the fundamental concept in yet another way: people do things because they hear words that make them do things, and effective leaders say the right words, in the right ways, at the right time, and thus take the single most powerful force known to mankind, and channel it in the direction of their choosing.

But first, let's start with one of the most clear-cut, irrefutable, undeniably obvious examples of the communication of leadership channeling the single most powerful force known to man in the direction of a bold leader's choosing.

DEPRESSION AND POVERTY

Let's turn back the clock to October 24, 1929. The day America broke. The day the unthinkable happened. The day the seeds were sown for the greatest example of the communication of leadership known to man to manifest itself in plain sight, though nearly nobody then or now would see it.

But most importantly: the day the spirit of the proudest country on Earth was shattered, in the absence of a leader who could use the communication of leadership to repair it. Until Franklin Delano Roosevelt came around, that is. But we'll talk about him after we talk about how bad it was.

One day it was fine. The American dream was real. *Americanism*, the sheer spirit of optimistic, industrious, innovative, and hard-working freedom was alive and well. One of the youngest countries was also one of the strongest. The entire world was surprised – in fact, shocked – by this rags-to-riches story.

The next day that all changed. The country went from riches to rags, and the man who brought it back to riches with the communication of leadership would earn four terms in the White House.

But let me be clear. It was very bad. It was a monumental disaster. It was a tangible mess, but more importantly, America's once-proud people lost their pride. In other words: the tangible disaster was second to the mental disaster that ensued when an entire nation lost touch with the most powerful force known to man.

KEY INSIGHT:

Defeat People's Unjustified Self-Doubt and Unearned Cynicism.

OUR ENVIRONMENTS SHAPE US, AND WE SHAPE THEM

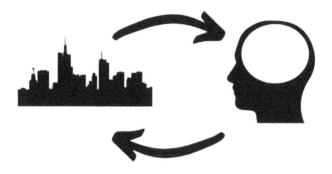

FIGURE 2: Our environment shapes us, and we shape our environment, which shapes us yet further in an ongoing cycle. We are both the architect of our environment and the product of it.

Mind you: the depression sprung from the minds of men. Sixteen million shares lost their value because their owners panicked and lost faith in the economy. What's the story there? Disaster in the human spirit first, and then as a result in the tangible realm. Innovation stagnated because people lost faith in the economy's ability to reward new inventions. Again, disaster in the human spirit first, and then as a result in the tangible realm.

The entire country suffered, struggling under a mountain of economic faithlessness, suffocating under the stifling weight of a deep disbelief in itself, that grew every moment it was left unaddressed. Make no mistake: this started, as all things do, in the minds of human beings, and was brought into existence by the negative actions that negative thoughts inevitably produce.

But let's talk about you. What would your odds during this time have looked like? You have a 25% chance of getting fired. But let's say you're not one of those people. You have a near 100% chance of seeing your wages cut, or your hours shortened. No movies, no fancy food, no new clothes, and for many people, no food, fancy or otherwise. A sense of uselessness; of ennui; of pure anxiety. Dark, dreary dread that penetrates everything sprouts in the cracks of the broken American spirit like a weed, and pervades even those with perfect equanimity.

"Oh, but I'm a professional, like a lawyer, or a doctor, so I would have been fine, right?" "But Peter! I'm a highly valued manager at a successful firm; surely I would be okay, right?" Nope. You can expect a 40% cut in your income. Imagine that today. One day, you're doing okay, maybe making $100,000 a year. Tomorrow? You're making $60,000.

Banks are breaking down. The entire financial system is underwater. People are walking for hundreds of miles to find any employment, and still coming back to their desperate families empty-handed.

Imagine suddenly not being able to provide for your family after decades of financial competence. Imagine financial security instantly turning into financial despair. Imagine this happening not to one person or one handful of people, but to an entire country, and not gradually, but in the blink of an eye.

The United States of America was silently screaming for a leader who could replace the faithlessness at the root of the Great Depression with an unwavering belief. A leader who could control the attention of the country *en masse*, direct it to a definite purpose of economic resurrection, produce intentional action toward that purpose, support that action with correct thinking, and supply a powerful motive to drive the action.

And that's exactly what it took. Now, we turn to Franklin Delano Roosevelt, the man who manifested the greatest economic resurrection known to man with the communication of leadership.

ELATION AND RICHES

I will tell you exactly how depression and poverty turned to elation and riches. A bold leader, Franklin Delano Roosevelt, used the communication of leadership to channel the most powerful force known to man to the worthy end of resurrecting the United States. So, how did he do it? Let's select one example: fireside chats.

He controlled attention by entering the homes of everyone who would listen with the power of radio, and by *creating a counterfactual simulation*, and *addressing the people's pain* (two strategies you'll learn).

He directed this controlled attention in the direction of the goal of resurrecting the United States with *vision-sharing* and *belief-transfer*.

He created intentional action on a mass-scale with *social-proof-pacing* and *plan-projecting*. Short-sighted historians who do not attribute the economic revival to FDR's communication, and only to his tangible plans, forget that those plans rely on opt-in from confident citizens, which can only be achieved with *communication*.

He supported intentional action with correct thinking by *super-ego-appeals* and *value-invocations*.

He provided a powerful motive to empower the entire process with *benefit-of-benefit statements* and *broken-justice reparations*.

When he repaired the spirit of America, when he reconnected people with the single most powerful force known to man, the whole story changed. It was rags to riches again.

Virtually every single historian agrees on the importance of the mindset shift in producing the economic shift. But you won't find a historian, or anyone, who understands the hidden components of the communication of leadership that created that mindset shift in the first place. Until now.

But why does this matter today? For this reason: in the story of every single organization, in every single voluntary association of human beings, whether it is a fortune-500 company of 100,000 employees or a small, scrappy startup of ten, you will find some element of the story of this country during the depression. In other words: every single "mastermind," whether it is ten people, 100,000, or an entire country, faces problems and looks to leaders to solve them. The legendary leaders that succeed do so by reconnecting the members of the mastermind to the single most powerful force known to man. And they do that by communicating in a certain way.

And here's my question to you: Will you be one of them?

ARE THESE STRATEGIES ACCIDENTS?

Message-hacking is the art of identifying powerful language produced by legendary leaders and reverse-engineering the sources of its impact, allowing you to wield the same influence yourself. But the question remains: Are these strategies intentional, or are they accidents?

My first answer is that it doesn't matter. We know the techniques are there. We know how to replicate them. We know their immense power, and why they have such strength. Whether or not the leader put them there intentionally or by accident is, in light of all this, secondary.

My second answer is that I firmly believe they are almost entirely intentional. Of course, it's impossible to know for sure, but we can reasonably conclude that intent is there.

First, the messages we study are all of massive consequence. Imagine you are about to address a nation in a time of immense crisis. Maybe you are addressing the United States during the Cuban missile crisis, and a pervasive (and realistic) fear that the cold war might turn hot and annihilate nearly all of humanity dominates your country. Or maybe you are a political ideologue, convinced that the other side in power will spell disaster for the United States, sowing the downfall of our Republic, and you find yourself speaking on national television before the voting booths open. Or maybe you are addressing not a country, but an army on the eve of the largest sea-based invasion in the history of warfare. What are you not going to do? Wing it. You are going to make sure that every sentence, every word, every idea, every letter, every syllable, every implication, every connotation, every subtle vocal intonation, every pitch-change, and every single individual unit of meaning is perfectly suited to the task before you. Shirking this burden might spell disaster. And you didn't end up in this position of power by shirking your burdens and creating disasters, did you?

Second, the leaders we study have massive reserves of resources. Maybe if the leaders didn't have massive reserves of resources, I would believe they weren't so intentional with their messaging. I would think, "Sure, it would have been great if they could modulate their messaging to perfection, but they probably were too busy." But here's the key: These leaders have massive apparatuses behind them, backing them in the endeavor of crafting the perfect message. We're talking about armies of speech-writers, psychologists, advisers, and the finest political minds of their eras, all collaborating to guarantee perfection. If someone hires someone else to fill a job with a clear description of duties, those duties will be completed intentionally and deliberately, right?

Third, a developmental line connects messages over time. If we analyze history-moving messages all together, a clear developmental line connects them. They seem to echo each other's persuasive compositions, either drawing insights from the same pool of knowledge or from each other. In short, compelling evidence based on macro-analysis of these messages over time suggests that the leaders (and their teams) actually message-hacked the messages of the leaders who came before them, just like we will in this book.

And message-hacking, as we know, is a deliberate and intentional process.

Fourth, devoted personnel handled these messages. These messages were not created by someone pulled away from their main task and sent to do some work on the side. Can you imagine that? Can you imagine John F. Kennedy walking up to the White-house interior décor-officer and saying, "Hey, the furniture looks fine for now, so can you please take 30 minutes to write what I'm going to say to the nation regarding the possibility of impending nuclear doom?" The leaders we study know messaging is too important to conduct haphazardly. Instead, many of these leaders relied on qualified people hired specifically for the role of crafting messages.

Fifth, the leaders have learned. Remember the single quality making someone a leader? They persuade others to do positive things. And by virtue of this inherent duty of leadership, these leaders have honed incredibly powerful skills over the decades. They have determined exactly how to communicate in every situation; exactly how to inspire, impact, and influence with ease; exactly what to say and how to say it, or else they wouldn't have become leaders in the position to speak words we would study today. Thus, we can conclude, because they possessed a highly honed and intuitive mastery of influence and communication – the core tasks of leadership – they discovered deliberate techniques over the decades leading to the peak position in their careers, from which they leave behind the messages we analyze.

Sixth, they are too complicated and artistic to be random. This is most evident in aesthetic analysis, in which we determine the elements of the language itself making it so tremendously beautiful. Aesthetic analysis often reveals mathematically precise aspects of the language, arranged in uniquely powerful ways. And of course, improbable things happen all the time, but if you are going to bet on it, you would bet these deeply complex mathematical and geometric relationships between words didn't just happen randomly. You would bet someone intentionally created them that way. The law of entropy suggests that matter tends toward chaos, and energy has to be expended to order to arrange matter in useful and productive ways. Why? Because matter has a near-infinite set of possible arrangements, but only a tiny, infinitesimally small portion of these arrangements are useful to humans. Likewise, words have a near-infinite set of possible arrangements. Only a tiny portion of these possible arrangements are uniquely powerful, beautiful, and compelling to humans. And just like energy must be expended to arrange matter in ordered and useful ways, energy must be expended to arrange words in beautiful and compelling ways. Thus, it is deliberate and intentional.

Seventh, there is a knowledge-trail extending far into the past. We might think we are uniquely blessed with the foundational knowledge of the core fields fundamental to message-hacking, but a trail of understanding extends back thousands of years. We might think our modern understanding of evolutionary biology is necessary to discover the traits it hammered into human psychology; the traits that legendary communication appeals to. Indeed, it is particularly powerful today. But Charles Darwin published *The Origin of Species* in 1859 and Aristotle discovered the core rhetorical triad – emotion (pathos), logic (logos), and evidence (ethos) – around 2,000 years ago. This exemplifies how the leaders we study had a body of knowledge to deliberately and intentionally draw upon, just as we do. Ours is bigger, more reliable, and more refined, but this doesn't mean they were clueless.

Eighth, the task is inherently deliberate. Crafting a message often comes down to answering a series of questions, either implicitly and subconsciously or explicitly and consciously: "What is the benefit of doing this action for my audience? What's at stake if they don't? How can I grab attention?" In other words, you are intentionally creating something from nothing, not allowing a random process to take its arbitrary course and passively accepting the result.

There is a reason I go to such lengths to persuade you to see the intent behind the legendary words we will shortly begin to study. It is vastly more exciting and infinitely more meaningful to know, for example, that John F. Kennedy (and his team) specifically designed the message. When we assume intent behind the message, we almost come into contact with the leaders themselves, sitting before them in a lecture hall as they explain what they did, why they did it, and why it worked.

MESSAGE-HACKING VISUALIZED

FIGURE 3: This book is built around the process of analyzing a legendary speech, uncovering its strategies and tactics, packaging these strategies and tactics into a repeatable framework, collecting these frameworks in the manuscript, which you then read to learn the frameworks that you plug into your message, making it as effective as the legendary speech in which I discovered the strategy.

COMMUNICATION ALGORITHMS VISUALIZED

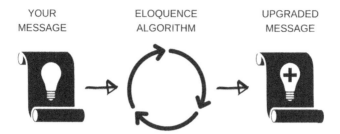

FIGURE 4: The strategies revealed in this book act as repeatable step-by-step algorithms. Provide the input parameters – your language – and run the algorithm to produce an upgraded version of the input.

MASTERY VISUALIZED

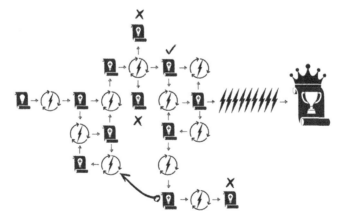

FIGURE 5: Communication mastery is the result of chaining these algorithms together.

..............................Chapter Summary...............................

- There is a little-known but deeply powerful force available to all, capable of performing the miraculous.
- The legendary leaders of history, like Franklin Delano Roosevelt, Mahatma Gandhi, and John F. Kennedy used it.
- It is human attention centered on a definite purpose backed by action, correct thinking, and a powerful motive.
- Legendary leaders produce legendary results by communicating in such a way that they harness this force.
- Ineffective leaders typically fail to use this force. They produce mediocre results due to this failure.
- This book exemplifies the strategy of message-hacking, which reverse-engineers the words of legendary leaders.

KEY INSIGHT:

The Legendary Words of Legendary Leaders Reveal the Secrets of Legendary Language.

We Can Discover, Adopt, and Adapt These Principles to Serve Any Communication Purpose.

Claim These Free Resources that Will Help You Unleash the Power of Your Words and Speak with Confidence. Visit www.speakforsuccesshub.com/toolkit for Access.

18 Free PDF Resources

12 Iron Rules for Captivating Story, 21 Speeches that Changed the World, 341-Point Influence Checklist, 143 Persuasive Cognitive Biases, 17 Ways to Think On Your Feet, 18 Lies About Speaking Well, 137 Deadly Logical Fallacies, 12 Iron Rules For Captivating Slides, 371 Words that Persuade, 63 Truths of Speaking Well, 27 Laws of Empathy, 21 Secrets of Legendary Speeches, 19 Scripts that Persuade, 12 Iron Rules For Captivating Speech, 33 Laws of Charisma, 11 Influence Formulas, 219-Point Speech-Writing Checklist, 21 Eloquence Formulas

Claim These Free Resources that Will Help You Unleash the Power of Your Words and Speak with Confidence. Visit <u>www.speakforsuccesshub.com/toolkit</u> for Access.

30 Free Video Lessons

We'll send you one free video lesson every day for 30 days, written and recorded by Peter D. Andrei. Days 1-10 cover authenticity, the prerequisite to confidence and persuasive power. Days 11-20 cover building self-belief and defeating communication anxiety. Days 21-30 cover how to speak with impact and influence, ensuring your words change minds instead of falling flat. Authenticity, self-belief, and impact – this course helps you master three components of confidence, turning even the most high-stakes presentations from obstacles into opportunities.

Claim These Free Resources that Will Help You Unleash the Power of Your Words and Speak with Confidence. Visit www.speakforsuccesshub.com/toolkit for Access.

2 Free Workbooks

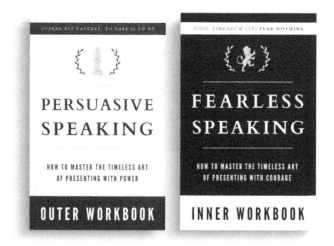

We'll send you two free workbooks, including long-lost excerpts by Dale Carnegie, the mega-bestselling author of *How to Win Friends and Influence People* (5,000,000 copies sold). *Fearless Speaking* guides you in the proven principles of mastering your inner game as a speaker. *Persuasive Speaking* guides you in the time-tested tactics of mastering your outer game by maximizing the power of your words. All of these resources complement the Speak for Success collection.

SPEAK FOR SUCCESS COLLECTION BOOK

XIII

THE LANGUAGE OF LEADERSHIP CHAPTER

II

DURING WAR:

Dwight D. Eisenhower's Invasion-Eve Address

"SOLDIERS, SAILORS, AND AIRMEN OF THE ALLIED EXPEDITIONARY FORCE..."

I MAGINE THIS. THE YEAR IS 1944. You're a young man. For years, you heard about the conflict raging in Europe. For years, you told yourself it would end before the United States would get involved.

It didn't.

And now you must pack your bags, say goodbye to your family, and arrive at a desolate training camp, suffocated by the hot dust of the American heartland. Training begins.

First, they make you suffer: thousands of pushups, and countless runs up mountains in the heat of the summer sun, carrying a 50-pound rucksack. The thick burlap of your uniform offers no respite from the sweltering heat.

Next, after you're hard as iron, after you're sharp as a tack, after the cruel and creative forms of suffering force you to shed every ounce of weakness from your soul, the focus shifts from gaining discipline to mastering the art of waging modern warfare.

They call you "three-month wonders." In three months, they turn you from an ordinary young man into an instrument of the finest fighting force the world has ever seen. You become a professional. You shed your old identity for a new one. Whatever you were before – a scientist, a teacher, a student, a farmer, a businessman – doesn't matter anymore. It's gone. You are a soldier; a warrior of the light, destined to fight one of the darkest evils the world has ever known: Nazi Germany.

You mastered squad tactics and strategy. You mastered your weapons. You mastered survival skills. Every technique, tactic, or maneuver you could possibly need to call upon in the heat of battle is second-nature to you. Your hand-to-hand combat is deadly, efficient, and precise. Your marksmanship is phenomenal. Wind, rain, range, and incoming fire can't sway your steady aim.

Despite this – despite the overpowering professionalism of the allied expeditionary force, despite its massive material and technical advantage, despite the surpassing devotion and courage of its personnel, despite the united support for the war effort on the home-front, despite the gains made by the United Kingdom in Africa, your own navy in the Pacific, and the Russians in the East – despite all this, you fear.

You fear defeat. You fear death. You fear the loss of everything you hold dear to your heart. You fear letting down your country. You fear the unknown. You come to fear fear itself; to fear losing the mental war between paralyzing fear and liberating courage.

You heard stories of the German lighting war, the Blitzkrieg, effortlessly toppling European Democracy after European Democracy. You heard about the sheer force of the German army's thrusts into Russia, taking 50 kilometers a day with relative ease. You know they fought around the world – the cold snow of Russia, the hedgerows of France, the mountains of Greece, the hot sands of Africa – with ruthless and unstoppable efficiency.

You know ideological fervor dominates these enemy soldiers; you know these men are fanatical in their devotion, tricked into believing they fight and die for the right cause by a propaganda machine so sophisticated, so compelling, and so powerful it can quickly distort any reality into an unrecognizable lie. And you know you might end up facing the *Volksturm:* the "people's army," comprised of ill-equipped and ill-trained young boys and old men, created in a final act of desperation.

You learned about their weapons in the training classrooms: Machines efficient, effective, and fearsome; machines of unparalleled strength; machines designed to gnaw at the sanity of their enemies, punching not only through military ramparts but tearing down psychological fortifications.

You heard how their armies captured hundreds of thousands in swift pincer movements, and how their generals are some of the best in the world. You heard how 300,000 men of the British expeditionary force crowded on the beach of Dunkirk like fish in a barrel escaped total annihilation by a hair, barely getting across the English Channel and just narrowly escaping certain death.

You know all this. You heard the stories. But you also know your own strength. You know the righteousness of your cause. You know the intensity of your power. And you know you will never give up. So, the questions run through your mind constantly: Who will prevail? Who will – as Franklin Delano Roosevelt said – win through to absolute victory? Will Nazi tyranny run the world? Or freedom? Will you return to your wife, your children, your house, your country as a victor? Or will you die a malnourished prisoner of war behind the bars of a cell in Germany? Will you answer the call of duty? Or will you find your reservoirs of courage lacking? What will you have to do? What will you have to see? What will happen to you? Will you be one of the lucky few? Or not? And if you die, will it have been in vain? Necessary? Unnecessary? The result of a foolish mistake? A devoted final stand?

Nothing can prepare a man for war. In the long days between the end of training and the start of deployment, fear ebbs into courage and back into fear again. Certainty turns into doubt, and doubt into detachment; detachment into equanimity, and equanimity back into fear the next time you hear a story of what's facing you across the Atlantic. One truth becomes clear to you: The only way you can win the war in the Atlantic is to win the war in your mind, and hope your brothers do the same.

Now, start imagining duty calls you to lead this army. Start imaging it is time to ask them to make the ultimate sacrifice. Start imagining you carry the responsibility of the entire ordeal squarely on your shoulders. Put yourself in the shoes of General Dwight D. Eisenhower.

You know one thing: The outcome of the war in Europe is inextricably, intrinsically, inalienably linked to the outcome of the war in the minds of your men; in the soul of your army; in the hearts of your warriors.

On the eve of the biggest military landing in the history of the world, you arrange to say a few short words to your men. Your goal? The same goal of any real leader: To help them win the war in their minds; to help them convert fear into courage, doubt into certainty, and apathy into purpose. What will you say?

PASSAGE #1:

Soldiers, Sailors, and Airmen of the Allied Expeditionary Force!

SECRET #1:

How to activate psychological self-identity for instant impact and influence.

Identity is everything. Humans see themselves in certain ways at certain times, and how we interact with the world expands, contracts, and morphs – often completely reversing if necessary – to match this identity. Identity can come from anywhere; it can be self-imposed, or drawn from the demands, expectations, and beliefs of others. We will fight – occasionally to the death – to preserve our identities.

And our identities contain sub-identities. At school, we are a student. At work, we are a professional. Spiritually, we typically identify with a group. Politically, we say "I am a..."

Identities can be abstract – "I am a caring person" – or specific: "I belong to X political party." Here is the key: At all times, one identity prevails, and the others lie latent. Lead people to behave in certain ways by emphasizing their preexisting sub-identity that acts how you want them to act. Emphasize whichever of their sub-identities is most persuasively advantageous, bringing it to the forefront, and activating it until it prevails and all other sub-identities lie latent. Remind people of the identity they hold that will lead them to act how you want them to; remind people that they are [insert identity], because they know that people who are [insert identity] act [insert behaviors – the behaviors lining up with what you want from them].

"I am an [insert identity], and [insert identity] does [insert actions]." This is the foundational formula of an identity statement.

Whether you realize it or not, at all times you are acting according to the mandates of such a statement, that you are an [insert identity]. And this only matters for one reason: Because people who are [insert identity] act like [insert code of action belonging to this identity]. This is the key.

HOW ATTRIBUTE SUBSTITUTION SHAPES OUR JUDGEMENTS

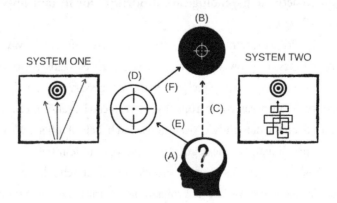

FIGURE 6: Cognitive substitution is foundational to many of these cognitive processes, both producing them and flowing from them. We cover it more deeply in a later section. When someone is prompted (A) to form an evaluation about a "target question" (B), they can either approach it logically, deliberately, and slowly with system

two (C) or perform "attribute substitution," which is a system one process. They "substitute" a "substitute question" (D) for the target question, evaluate this substitute question (E), and transfer the answer to the target question (F). This occurs in part because the substituted question is easier to evaluate than the target question. System one is the home of our rapid, cognitive-bias-driven thought processes, while system two is the home of our deliberate, effortful, and logical thought processes.

HOW IDENTITY-BASED PERSUASION HIJACKS SUBSTITUTION

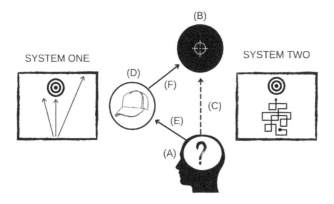

FIGURE 7: When someone is prompted (A) to form an evaluation about the question "how they should act" (B), they can either approach it logically, deliberately, and slowly with system two (C) or substitute the question "what does someone with my identity act?" (D) for the target question, evaluate this substitute question (E), and transfer the answer to the target question (F).

Leaders must inspire positive action. You want to be a leader. So, you must inspire positive actions. What better way to do it than by empowering the particular self-identity most likely to create those positive actions? Remember this mantra: Identity is the key to action.

This is why Eisenhower started by calling out the sub-identity conducive to getting these young men to think and do what he wanted them to think and do: "soldiers, sailors, and airmen..."

You are not an American in this moment. You are not a young man. You are not a patriot. You are not a student. Your national identity sinks to the bottom of your consciousness, just like these other sub-identities. In this moment, you are a soldier, a sailor, or an airman; and because this identity describes you, you suddenly begin to think like a soldier, a sailor, or an airman, and not any other sub-identity. This is exactly the kind of thinking Eisenhower wants to inspire. He started by activating the sub-identities of his audience members that inspire the kind of thinking most conducive to the rest of his message.

KEY INSIGHT:

Our Identity Shapes Our Behavior. And Identity Is Somewhat Flexible.

Speak to the Parts of People that Identify with Goodness, Virtue, Truth-Seeking, and Hope.

SECRET #2:

How to immediately activate evolutionary pressures with the proven power of psychological coalitions.

You might be surprised at the sheer amount of psychological persuasion tied to such a simple, seemingly commonplace opening. It gets even more complicated, and even more powerful. Eisenhower didn't just say, "soldiers, sailors, and airmen..." he said "soldiers, sailors, and airmen of the *Allied Expeditionary Force*."

Do those words seem inconsequential? Perhaps irrelevant? Like an afterthought? Think again. Those words carry immense power because they activate yet another type of identity: group identity; identity based around membership in a psychological coalition. Layered over the first invocation of a personal identity, this invocation of a group identity is tremendously powerful.

How do you alter the format of an identity statement, an often-implicit statement of one's primary identity in the moment, to include group identity too? Like so: It morphs from "I am an [insert identity], and [insert identity] does [insert actions]," to "I am an [insert identity] belonging to [insert group], and [insert identity] does [insert actions]."

Invoking personal identity is incredibly powerful, as is invoking group identity. Layering them over one another is a new level of persuasive force altogether. And it demonstrates that Eisenhower understood the critical element of psychological persuasion better than many of his colleagues; he understood the single secret of mass movements that achieve audacious goals against all the odds; he understood the persuasive power of a deeply ingrained, subconsciously hyperactive psychological state; he understood the power of psychological coalitions. We over me and you. Together over apart. For each other over for ourselves.

The psychology of teams is one of the most persuasive, influential forces known to humanity. It truly is none other than the mastermind principle mentioned in the foreword. The human psychology is thrilled by team-member status. It's scientific and evolutionary. Humans who were pleased by being a part of a team were more likely to form a team, and about 1,000,000 years ago, being in a team was the difference between life and death, so the gene controlling whether or not someone is pleased by team status was naturally selected to be passed on through the generations, until today, when leaders can play upon that gene; when leaders can use the very fabric of our DNA in their favor, in our favor, and in the world's favor.

So, the science is clear: The mechanism of evolution makes human beings want, at times above all else, to belong to a larger coalition of human beings. We know, and perhaps have experienced firsthand, how pleasing team status can be.

When people enter a coalition, they abandon reservations and throw themselves with renewed vigor to the pursuit of a goal. The tribal psychology of teams gives people self-identity, a belief system that organizes the world in neat little ways, and a self-reinforcing cycle of intellectual confirmation. It creates a comfortable nook of common belief, common vision, common goal, common enemy, common identity, and common struggle.

Team psychology has massive appeal to our 1,000,000-year-old brains, and thus holds massive influence over us. Furthermore, building coalitions around transformative aspirations increases the likelihood of both the success of the coalition and the actualization of the aspiration.

How does Eisenhower build a coalition to influence, control attention, and achieve persuasive force? Specifically, how does he build a coalition around transformative aspirations?

"Soldiers, sailors, and airmen of the Allied Expeditionary Force."

Coalition? Check. Transformation? Check. Team psychology activated? Check. Attention controlled? Check.

Everyone wants to be a smaller part of something bigger than themselves. A good coalition is greater than the sum of its parts, and everyone wants to be elevated by the power of a team. It is one of the dualities of human desires. We want to balance individualism with our role as a valued part of a group.

KEY INSIGHT:

We Don't Want the Terror of Unsupported Individualism or the Constriction of a Uniform Group.

We Seek a Balance Between "Alone" and "Never Alone;" "Too Free" and "Not Free Enough."

SECRET #3:

How to guarantee a positive reception by appealing to the primacy effect.

The primacy effect is that what we first perceive colors our perception of what comes after. We overweigh information we discern first. If we feel good about someone because they presented the quality of empathy when we first met, we overweigh this positive first impression and stick to it even after discerning disconfirming information later on.

Due to the primacy effect, you must choose your starting words carefully. They are make-or-break. They set expectations. Everything you say after will be seen through the lens of your first words. It's brutally unavoidable. But if you master the art of the start, it will be brutally effective, working wonders in your favor.

THE LITTLE-KNOWN PSYCHOLOGY OF FIRST IMPRESSIONS

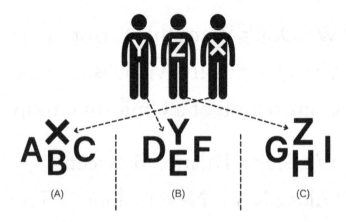

FIGURE 8: The audience perceives three people. The first person portrays quality Y. The audience has a mental category that includes items with the quality Y (B). Items in this category also have qualities D, E, and F. The audience lumps the first person into this category, transmuting the qualities D, E, and F to them. The second portrays quality Z, and he gets lumped into a category that transmutes the qualities G, H, and I to him (C) – qualities he never portrayed. Person X portrays quality X. You know the story: Now, he is not only a person who portrayed X, but a member of a mental category that includes the un-portrayed qualities A, B, and C (A), which the audience now transmutes onto him. This is a form of influence by mere association.

Eisenhower's opening was brutally effective, because by invoking not one but two forms of identity – the personal identity and the group identity – he immediately created the most compelling opening possible; one that grabbed attention, established appropriate context, set high expectations, and colored everything he said afterwards through the lens of "I am a soldier of the Allied Expeditionary Force."

SECRET #4:

How to reliably inspire people to act in positive ways with the little-known principle of persuasive consistency.

In his groundbreaking book *Influence: The Psychology of Persuasion*, Robert Cialdini presents six core elements of effective persuasion: scarcity, consensus, authority, reciprocity, likeability, and consistency. In this section, we address consistency.

Charlie Munger, billionaire investor and partner to Warren Buffet, also gave reference to this element of human psychology in his famous Harvard commencement address titled *The Psychology of Human Misjudgment*, which he updated and expanded in his book *Poor Charlie's Almanack*. While Cialdini refers to this psychological tendency as the consistency (or commitment) principle, Munger calls it the inconsistency avoidance tendency. This is what he said in the famous address about this powerful psychological force: "One corollary of Inconsistency-Avoidance Tendency is that a person making big sacrifices in the course of assuming a new identity will intensify his devotion to the new identity. After all, it would be quite inconsistent behavior to make a large sacrifice for something that was no good. And thus civilization has invented many tough and solemn initiation ceremonies, often public in nature, that intensify new commitments made. While Inconsistency-Avoidance Tendency, with its 'status quo bias,' immensely harms sound education, it also causes much benefit. For instance, a near-ultimate inconsistency would be to teach something to others that one did not believe true. And so, in clinical medical education, the learner is forced to 'see one, do one, and then teach one,' with the teaching pounding the learning into the teacher. Of course, the power of teaching to influence the cognition of the teacher is not always a benefit to society. When such power flows into political and cult evangelism, there are often bad consequences. For instance, modern education often does much damage when young students are taught dubious political notions and then enthusiastically push these notions on the rest of us. The pushing seldom convinces others. But as students pound into their mental habits what they are pushing out, the students are often permanently damaged. Educational institutions that create a climate where much of this goes on are, I think, irresponsible. It is important not to thus put one's brain in chains before one has come anywhere near his full potentiality as a rational person."

To put it simply, people tend to avoid acting inconsistently with past actions. This comes from our innate human desire to limit confusion and conserve cognitive resources by organizing the world in artificially neat ways, in which we always acted correctly (meaning that there's no need to be inconsistent with our past selves). We also conserve mental resources by saying "I probably thought this action through the first time, so this time, I'll trust my past-self."

You can use this powerful component of human in psychology by conveying consistency indicators: statements tying previous audience actions to your proposed action. Make it seem like doing what you want would be consistent with their history of related actions: "You've probably always done [insert related action; the basis for consistency]. The truth is that [insert your proposal] is essentially continuing this history of positive action, because..."

HOW TO INFLUENCE WITH THE CONSISTENCY PRINCIPLE

FIGURE 9: When evaluating a new option, people will be much more likely to accept it if it is consistent with their history of related actions.

In this opening, Eisenhower implied consistency. We already discussed the opening as an outstanding example of invoking identity. But every identity invocation inherently activates the consistency principle, because it implies a history of actions and thoughts consistent with the ones Eisenhower wants to inspire. If your identity is "soldier," acting courageously, following orders with discipline, and receiving the rest of the message with a mindset of bravery is consistent. And as we know, people can't resist leaping to the call of consistency, and jumping away from even the slightest signal of inconsistency. Not only did this opening invoke identity, it also activated consistency. "I'm a soldier. Listening to the rest of this message in a spirit of courage is consistent with who I am."

SECRET #5:

How to avoid subconsciously confusing messaging by using the art of contextual pre-framing.

Compare the following two sentences.

"The global extreme poverty rate is 10%."

"The global extreme poverty rate is only 10%."

And compare these two sequences of sentences.

"The international economic system is bad. The global extreme poverty rate is 10%.

"The international economic system is good. The global extreme poverty rate is 10%."

These two comparisons illustrate pre-framing. In the first comparison, the word "only" preceded the statistic in the second sentence. This word subtly implies the number is relatively small. Even though the two sentences convey the same exact information, simply by adding this one word, the second sentence casts the information in a positive light, while the first is either ambiguous or negative. The word is meaningless. 10% is equal to "only" 10%.

In the second comparison, the two sentences conveying the statistic itself are identical. But what comes before them pre-frames each sentence differently, suggesting a different interpretation.

The pre-framing is clear. Item one suggests a mindset, and this mindset leads to a particular interpretation of item two. Simply by changing what comes before an item, you can foster two completely opposite interpretations of the same item.

In the first comparison, "only" (item one) pre-framed 10% (item two). Item two remained identical in both sentences. Item one suggested a mindset through which to interpret the following information. Thus, the sentiment of the message completely reversed. In the second comparison, item two ("The global extreme poverty rate is 10%") remained the same, but the pre-frames suggested different mindsets through which to view item two, leading to opposite interpretations.

Pre-framing is boundless. Even the reputation of the speaker can pre-frame information. For example, if you are known as a status-quo optimist who believes the incremental progress of the world is positive and the system fostering it should be preserved, you can say, "the global extreme poverty rate is 10%" and your reputation will pre-frame this sentiment as positive. On the other hand, if you are an anti-status quo rebel who wants to institute a new international economic system, and if people understand this about you – if you have a reputation – it can pre-frame the same exact sentence, that "the global extreme poverty rate is 10%," as an incrimination of the system's failure.

Anchoring can be conceived as a form of pre-framing as well. The anchoring effect is our tendency for the first number we hear (the anchor) to irrationally influence us. We reach an inaccurate judgement by starting at the anchor and insufficiently adjusting either downward or upward.

THE ANCHORING EFFECT VISUALIZED

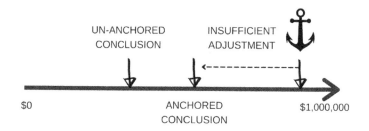

FIGURE 10: An anchor set at a high value becomes the starting point of your evaluation. You begin at the anchor and adjust from it in the appropriate direction, but do so insufficiently. In this example, this leaders to a higher anchored conclusion. Your un-anchored conclusion would have been lower. This is in favor of the "anchorer."

The anchoring effect functions through the following characteristics of human psychology: perceptual relativity, comparative perception, directional judgement, insufficient adjustment, and primacy.

What is perceptual relativity? All our judgements form relative to other perceptions we have. Is it good or bad that we have a 10% global extreme poverty rate? Most will have a difficult time answering with certainty. Why? Perception is relative, and this statistic lacks a point of reference. What about this? 20 years ago, we had a global extreme poverty rate of 40%. Now, it's 10%. In this case, the perception is typically positive: "Yes, that's fairly good." Why? 10% is low relative to the rest of the information, namely that it was once 40%. (Fun fact: It was once 99.9999% prior to the industrial revolution).

PERCEPTUAL RELATIVITY VISUALIZED

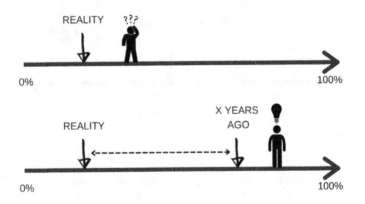

FIGURE 11: Humans struggle to judge reality in a perceptual vacuum. We need points of comparison. If we are judging "how good reality is now," we often find ourselves confused. We lack relativity. The statement of "how bad reality was X years ago" provides it.

What is comparative perception? Our judgements are based on comparison between alternatives. People are happy to earn $60,000 a year if their closest co-worker earns $55,000, but unhappy if their closest co-worker earns $65,000. Isn't $60,000 equal to $60,000, no matter what someone else earns? Of course, but that's not how human perception and judgement work. We can't judge a single item unless we have a point of comparison. And once we find a point of comparison, it becomes our anchor, against which we measure subsequent items.

COMPARATIVE PERCEPTION VISUALIZED

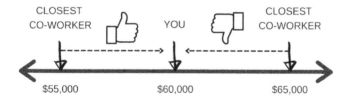

FIGURE 12: Humans struggle to judge reality in a perceptual vacuum. We need points of comparison. If we are judging "how good reality is now," we often find ourselves confused. We lack relativity. The statement of "how bad reality was X years ago" provides it.

What is directional judgment? We are more concerned with the direction of trends rather than their magnitude. We are more concerned with the direction of the jump from our salary to that of our closest co-worker, and if it is a jump up or a jump down. We don't care so much about the size of the jump. This is part of why we overweigh the initial anchor: We care if subsequent numbers are higher or lower, but not how much so. We know that we want to negotiate downward (direction) from an excessively high price in a negotiation, but by how much (magnitude)? We decide magnitude by adjustment from an anchor.

DIRECTIONAL JUDGMENT VISUALIZED

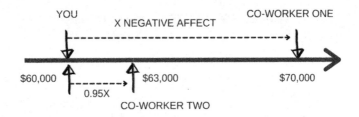

FIGURE 13: We overweigh direction compared to magnitude. If we earn $60,000 a year and a close co-worker earns $70,000 a year, this produces "X" negative affect; "X" negative emotion. If a second close co-worker earns $63,000 a year, this is 10% less than the first co-worker, but produces 95% of the negative emotional impact; that is, only 5% less emotional impact. This is a hypothetical example with hypothetical numbers, but it mirrors experimental evidence. It shows us that direction influences our emotions more than magnitude. If our closest co-worker makes more than us, that "directional" fact alone influences us more than facts related to magnitude; than facts related to the size of the disparity.

What is insufficient adjustment? Insufficient adjustment impacts number-related estimations. This is how anchors influence us. It follows this process: The first number we encounter roots itself in our memory, and it becomes an anchor. Next, based on our interests, we begin to negotiate in the direction we seek, but determine the extent of our renegotiation by starting at the anchor and adjusting downward, often by an insufficient amount.

Consider this example. "This car, our newest model, is worth $200,000," says the agent. This prompts you to make a judgement: "How much do I think this lower-end SUV is worth?" Instead of starting over, we begin our valuation at the anchor, and adjust accordingly. In this case, we adjust downward from $200,000. "$100,000? Too much. $80,000? Still too much. $60,000? Getting there. $40,000? Seems about right." What's the problem? We often adjust insufficiently, resulting in a higher valuation than if we didn't see the anchor at all. If we first saw a lower anchor, $20,000, we would have insufficiently adjusted upward, perhaps landing at $30,000.

KEY INSIGHT:

Our Nervous Systems Take in an Incalculable Number of Inputs, Consciously and Unconsciously.

Judgment is the Result of Reason Acting On These Inputs, As Well As Past (And Anticipated) Inputs.

What is the primacy effect? The primacy effect is our tendency to overweigh the first information we encounter. Why does the primacy effect occur? Because of two features of psychology. The first? We take new evidence as confirmation of old conclusions (or primary conclusions – the first ones we make). This is confirmation bias. The second? We evaluate new information by comparing it to what we first learned. We can't judge a 10% extreme poverty rate on its own as easily as when we compare it to what we heard first: 40%.

THE PRIMACY EFFECT VISUALIZED

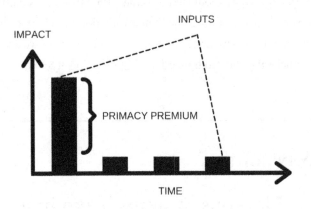

FIGURE 14: All else equal, the first item we perceive impacts us more than subsequent items. We may refer to this increased impact as the primacy premium.

When you are online shopping and see a high price crossed out next to a lower price, they are trying to anchor you to the high price. If the "retail price" is $1,000, but they are offering you the product for $500, you insufficiently adjust downward from $1,000 when evaluating the true worth. Perhaps you insufficiently adjust downward to $750, a higher number than $500, which makes the $500 price seem more attractive.

In *Win Bigly*, Scott Adams presents an example of unrelated anchoring. What does he suggest? If you are negotiating a price, at the beginning of the meeting, talk about some random person spending an exorbitant amount of money on a yacht (like $2,000,000). This will anchor your prospect to $2,000,000, and they will insufficiently adjust downward and probably offer more for your product. Anchors need only to be somewhere in the same neighborhood as the range of appropriate values. The $2,000,000 anchor will exert more influence if the range of appropriate values is somewhere between $1,000,000 and $1,500,000. You can't use a $2,000,000 anchor to raise the price paid for a $10 product. The $2,000,000 anchor is so absurdly far out of the appropriate range of evaluation that the prospect readily discards it.

Does anchoring in this manner work even if your product isn't a yacht? Yes, and this is the reason why this model of anchoring is called unrelated anchoring. Anchors work even if the first number describes a completely different item. Anchors work even if the high anchor you set describes the price of a yacht and you're selling a house. This is how desperately our minds scramble for information we can use to form comparisons. It's a shortcut we use to save mental resources. Since comparison-based decision-making is easy, we irrationally select a point of comparison, and we do this subconsciously and unknowingly.

Anchoring expresses the immense power of pre-framing. Imagine that you are walking to a conference on global poverty, and you see a sign saying "1%" through the corner of your eye. It doesn't even consciously register. You are not even aware you saw it. But nonetheless, it subconsciously pre-frames, acting as an item one, just waiting for a compatible item two it can color your interpretation of. When you hear the actual global rate of 10%, the 1% pre-frame anchors your perception, making you see the 10% as abysmal by the mechanism of insufficient adjustment. If you saw a 20% sign, it would be a different story. And remember, this is all occurring outside of your awareness.

We can (and should) expound and break down the concept of pre-framing, as we just did, but we must always remember the simplicity at its core: pre-framing is simply presenting an item creating whatever mindset will lead people to the interpretation you want them to apply to the second item; the item you are about to present.

In Eisenhower's case, his second item was the message enshrined in the rest of his speech. And what better way to pre-frame the message than by reminding them of their identity as soldiers? What better mindset to have when hearing the rest of the speech than one of bravery and dedication?

Now, I'm not saying Eisenhower knew exactly what I wrote in these pages; I'm not saying he had a definition of pre-framing the way we do, or was even aware of these techniques and frameworks.

Instead, he was simply using a best practice; one emerging through lessons from history, rhetorical tradition, and cultural evolution. I explained why it works and how to replicate the effect. Eisenhower just followed his intuition; an intuition informed by what those before him did that worked.

SECRET #6:

How to immediately command complete attention in this increasingly distracted world.

I recently saw a captivating Facebook Ad. I clicked through to the landing page, and there was a pre-headline that read: "Attention: Businessmen, Entrepreneurs, and the Self-Employed."

And it got my attention because, directly and authoritatively, it called out the group to which I belong. The same exact principle plays a role in the opening of this (and nearly every other) legendary message. When you use such a callout, it animates your presence in a compelling way. When you see your friend across the room and shout his name, two things happen without fail: you grab his attention and he listens to what you have to say.

Eisenhower's opening appealed to the same principle. He was able to captivate attention by calling out the audience directly. It's such a simple, commonplace, and even lackluster strategy. And yet, countless leaders speak to people who aren't even listening because they forgot to authoritatively grab their attention.

PASSAGE #2:

You are about to embark upon the Great Crusade, toward which we have striven these many months. The eyes of the world are upon you. The hope and prayers of liberty-loving people everywhere march with you. In company with our brave Allies and brothers-in-arms on other Fronts, you will bring about the destruction of the German war machine, the elimination of Nazi tyranny over the oppressed peoples of Europe, and security for ourselves in a free world.

SECRET #7:

How to use the sacred-profane spectrum to meet high-stakes moments appropriately.

We can't go far in our studies of communication theory and message-hacking without running across the idea of spectrums. It's simple: On one end, you have one quality; on the other end, you have the opposite quality. As you more from one end to the other, you have less of the quality you're moving away from, and more of the one you're moving toward. In the middle, it balances both; on either side, you have all of one and none of the other.

The spectrum between the sacred and the profane plays out in nearly every single message we hack. Ask yourself: Why do these leaders dress these messages up in such powerful, flowing, eloquent language? Why do they use language not suited for the everyday? Why don't they just speak in the vernacular? Why don't they just speak like they speak to their friends?

The answer is straightforward: They intuitively want to create a sense of the sacred. They want to subconsciously and subtly suggest their message is a clarion call to action from a higher plane of existence, even coming from God using the speaker as a vessel.

Sacred is defined as "Something dedicated or set apart for the service or worship of a deity or considered worthy of spiritual respect or devotion; or inspiring awe or reverence among believers. The property is often ascribed to objects, or places." Profane is defined as "Relating or devoted to that which is not sacred or biblical; secular rather than religious." Remember, the profane end of the spectrum does not describe a message defined by "bad words," or delivered in a seemingly disrespectful manner. This is a common misconception.

Now, this spectrum doesn't demand religion. On the sacred end of the spectrum, the message is dressed in language conveying a sense of respect, devotion, awe, reverence, and higher purpose; language subconsciously suggesting the subject is not commonplace, but a once-in-a-lifetime call to action. On the profane end of the spectrum, the message is dressed in language conveying a sense of everyday nonchalance; it's not disrespectful, but it's not reverent either.

To give you a quick example of the two ends of this spectrum, I saw two ads in a magazine. I will paraphrase them to the best of my ability. The first tried to hook me like this: "Want to be a better husband? Father? Leader? Want to connect to the well-spring of power within you, accomplish your God-given mission on this planet, and leave behind a lasting legacy?" The text was set under an image of the advertiser holding his three-year-old daughter in his arms.

The second tried this: "Want more money?" The text was set under an image of cash. The first oozed a sense of higher purpose, calling me to rise up and begin a journey inspiring reverence, awe, and devotion; a journey of significance. The second oozed a sense of nothing, really. It promised me something secular, tangible, physical; it gave me a purpose, but I could not say it was a higher purpose.

Which one is better? It depends. It depends on your circumstances, your audience, and yourself. Do you feel honest creating a sense of the sacred? Does it match the gravity and seriousness of your subject? Or are you stretching sacred language to fit a profane, everyday subject? Mismatching sacred language to a profane subject or profane language to a sacred subject is a common and significant blunder. They have to synergize. Countless messages fail for this particular reason: They try to paint a picture of a sacred subject with profane language or, just as commonly, they try to describe the profane with language befitting the sacred.

KEY INSIGHT:

To Speak Profanely About the Sacred and Reverently About the Profane Is a Major Mistake.

How Do You Avoid It? Convey the Unimportant Casually and the Important Formally.

VISUALIZING THE SACRED-PROFANE SPECTRUM

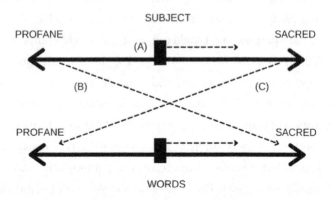

FIGURE 15: Make your words more sacred by identifying and elucidating the sacred aspects of your subject (A). Do not speak about a profane subject with sacred words (B) or a sacred subject with profane words (C).

If your subject lies on the middle of the spectrum, so too must your communication. Match it. And if you want to move further toward the sacred end of the spectrum, do so by further elucidating the sacredness of your subject. You must dig deep, and find the truth: "This subject of mine, what is it really? What are the consequences of it? Is it irrelevant to the lives of the people around me? Or can it change them for the better? Is there a higher purpose hidden here? Can I extract it, expand upon it, and explain it?"

If you answer yes, you know which end of the spectrum to move toward. And remember: It's a spectrum, so you don't have to go all the way there.

How do you create a sense of the sacred? Well, we are message-hacking, aren't we? So, the better question is this: How does Eisenhower?

If you're listening to a message, whether you're reading it or hearing it, and you find yourself in a mood of agape wonder, pondering something of high consequence, contemplating a journey upward to the accomplishment of a higher purpose, the message used sacred language. You are supposed to feel heavy-hearted; you are supposed to feel appropriately heavy-hearted, matching the seriousness of the subject before you, and the gravity of its consequences.

And how can you create this mood? Let's break down some of the sentence-level structures Eisenhower used.

You can tell them they are about to begin a journey, using a word for journey connoting high-stakes and higher purpose, like so: "You are about to embark upon *the Great Crusade...*"

You can reference the sheer amount of human effort your audience already devoted to the cause: "...toward which we have striven *these many months.*"

You can let them know there's a massive spotlight on them: "The eyes of the world are upon you."

You can tell them how the people they are doing this for, who are watching them in nervous anticipation, are rooting for them with every fiber of their souls: "The hope and prayers of liberty-loving people everywhere march with you."

You can show them they aren't alone, but part of a group – a psychological coalition – striving toward the goal with them: "In company with our brave Allies and brothers-in-arms on other Fronts..."

You can reference the goal itself, and if the goal is indeed a high-stakes higher purpose, you can just state it flatly (because it won't sound flat): "...you will bring about the destruction of the German war machine."

You can call out the morality of the journey. Nothing indicates the sacred like a moral endeavor, like the defeat of an evil: "...the elimination of Nazi tyranny..."

You can emphasize the higher human stakes by describing the suffering of the victims in the situation, who you are protecting: "...over the oppressed peoples of Europe..."

You can pepper the entire message with words connoting the sacred: "You are about to *embark upon* the *Great Crusade*, toward which we have *striven* these many months. The *eyes of the world* are upon you. The *hope and prayers* of *liberty-loving* people everywhere *march* with you. In company with our *brave* Allies and *brothers-in-arms* on other Fronts, you will bring about the destruction of the German war machine, the elimination of Nazi *tyranny* over the *oppressed* peoples of Europe, and *security* for ourselves in a *free world.*"

And finally, you can identify the value-driven benefit which dives deep to the inherent benefit of the surface benefit and hits upon core values (for example, not "more money," but the result of more money; "financial freedom and peace of mind"): "...and security for ourselves in a free world."

Message-hacking teaches us universal insights we can use in any communication situation. You might be questioning the relevance of the sacred-profane spectrum to your life. I'll show you an illuminating example. We can adapt this secret of the sacred and the profane to an everyday situation. You can use it to craft the marketing message for an investing course, for example.

There's a step zero. Analyze the situation. Analyze it deeply and thoroughly. And keep going at it until you find a source of the sacred to tap into; until you identify how the situation calls for a sacred message, or determine there's nothing sacred about it at all. You will be surprised by how much around us is sacred if you look at it under the right light.

Ask yourself: What are the stakes? What can this subject do for people? What consequences will it cause if they neglect it? What's the simple, straightforward, compelling moral narrative we can paint about this subject, one based on universally accepted values and principles?

It's not just a course. It's the key to peace of mind, to freedom, to the joy enabled by stress-free finances. We innately recognize how some things are sacred, like parenthood, or human potential, for example. Ask yourself: of these special subjects we innately find intrinsically sacred, which connect to your seemingly profane subject? Chances are it's more than one, meaning your subject is not profane at all, but fully sacred, if you paint it as such.

We'll discuss *re*framing (not *pre*-framing) later, but what you're really doing is reframing your subject according to this format: "It's not [insert profane description], it's [insert sacred description]."

It's not an investing course, it's freedom.

It's not a deadly and bloody war, it's a Great Crusade.

Step zero is fostering an understanding of the situation until you identified what makes it sacred, so you can create your statement of the sacred: "It's not [insert profane description], it's [insert sacred description]."

It works because it's real; it cuts through directly to the truth of the situation. It doesn't fabricate the sacred, it simply identifies the sacred that's already there, through careful observation, and points it out. It's not creating something; it's unveiling what has always been there.

Here's a secret within this secret: There are two lines of communication open between you and the people you're speaking to, not one. This is a big shocker to most people. And if this shocked you, there's a huge chance you missed tremendous opportunities because you didn't know what was possible when you use both lines of communication instead of falling back to only one.

The first line of communication is the direct; the words you say. They impart information directly to the conscious minds of your audience. The second line of communication is the subconscious.

The first is the explicit, the second is the implicit. The first is the direct, the second is the indirect. The second includes the subconscious and implicit messaging of your body language and vocal tonalities. But they also include the subtle implications of your spoken words. They include the subtext – the unspoken speech – layered under the words you actually say. And so much influence actually occurs in that sublayer. It's a shame if you neglect it.

UNDERSTANDING THE TWO KINDS OF COMMUNICATION

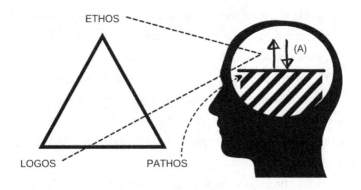

FIGURE 16: Influence occurs on both a conscious and subconscious (also called unconscious or non-conscious) level. The repetitive thoughts of the conscious mind influence the subconscious mind, while the state of the subconscious mind influences the conscious mind, often "tossing up" thoughts to the conscious mind. Some are great, some are distracting, some are nonsensical. Certain strategies are particularly suited for hitting at one of the two minds in particular: ethos and logos hit the conscious mind, while pathos tends to exert more influence over the subconscious mind. Use both.

And when you use the sacred end of the spectrum, no matter your individual circumstances or the specifics of your subject, the subconscious message sounds something like this: "You are being called to rise, manifest your innate human potential, and beat back the chaos of the world in its default state by exerting effort to order it in meaningful ways, improving your life, the lives of your family members, and the lives of all who will look at you as an example of what is possible. Will you answer the call? Or let it go unattended?"

If that's a power you want to tap into – moreover, to subconsciously tap into – now you know how.

KEY INSIGHT:

See the Deep and Abiding Meaning Behind the Seemingly Commonplace Surrounding Us.

Revealing the Hidden Miraculous Is One of the Greatest Gifts a Speaker Can Give An Audience.

Email Peter D. Andrei, the author of the Speak for Success collection and the President of Speak Truth Well LLC directly.

pandreibusiness@gmail.com

SECRET #8:

How to apply Aristotle's little-known 2,000-year-old key for effortlessly effective persuasion.

Emotion is everything. Thousands of sources over the past 2,000 years suggest people make decisions based on their emotions first, and then justify these emotional inclinations with logic.

Aristotle called it pathos. He broke down all persuasive language into three categories – three tools, if you will. The three tools? Pathos (emotion), ethos (evidence and the character of the speaker), and logos (logic).

ARISTOTLE'S 2,000-YEAR-OLD PERSUASIVE FRAMEWORK

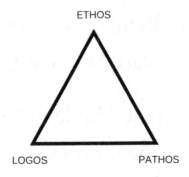

FIGURE 17: Thousands of years ago, Aristotle conveyed a timeless persuasive framework. He argued that all effective persuasion and impactful rhetoric was the result of successfully appealing to pathos (emotion), logos (logic), and ethos (evidence). Ethos has also been understood as a characteristic of the speaker: his credibility, character, and the extent to which he has the audience's interests at heart. This definition is valuable too.

You don't have to look very far to identify the primordial influence of emotions. And if it is indeed true that our emotions lead the way, then logos and ethos are the servants of pathos.

But here's the point: This isn't an inherently bad thing. Emotions serve a crucial role in our adaptation to life in an ambiguous world. To put it simply, our emotions can be broadly characterized into two big categories: good and bad. And when our ancestors were roaming through dangerous environments 1,000,000 years ago, and any wrong move could spell an instant and gruesome death, these two categories defined their actions by suggesting next steps: approach or avoid; fight or flight. If they felt anxious or afraid for any reason, this bad emotion suggested avoidance of a potential danger.

THE OBVIOUS TRUTH OF HUMAN COGNITION

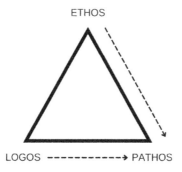

FIGURE 18: Many psychologists argue that ethos and logos are by default the servants of pathos, simply serving as ways to justify emotional judgements.

Emotions act as an internal survival mechanism. And emotions are informed by levels of higher intelligence our conscious minds can't access directly. Our subconscious minds pick up on significantly more inputs than our conscious minds do, and our emotions are shaped by this subconscious knowledge, by information we don't consciously know we have. Emotions can offer a window into a higher level of enlightenment regarding the situation we're in just as often as they can mislead us.

BREAKING DOWN HOW EMOTIONS SHAPE DECISIONS

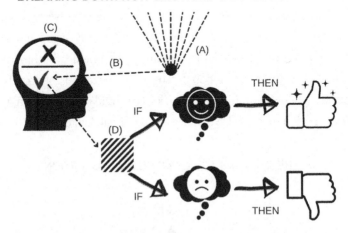

FIGURE 19: In a situation with many inputs (A) sent (B) to our minds (C), our subconscious (D) runs an emotional algorithm, establishing a decision on the basis of emotion.

So, how does Eisenhower use emotion in this passage? And how can we extrapolate a simple framework or broad insight from it? He sprinkles emotionally implicative words throughout; words inherently evoking certain emotions.

"You are about to *embark* upon the *Great Crusade*, toward which we have *striven* these many months. The *eyes of the world* are upon you. The *hope* and *prayers* of *liberty-loving people* everywhere *march* with you. In *company* with our *brave* Allies and *brothers-in-arms* on other Fronts, you will bring about the *destruction* of the German *war machine*, the *elimination* of *Nazi tyranny* over the *oppressed peoples* of Europe, and *security* for ourselves in a *free world.*"

Marketing calls these words trigger words, because they trigger a strong emotional pull from within. A strong internal force suddenly becomes your persuasive ally, either suggesting approaching you and your ideas, avoiding any alternatives, or both.

Just remember the big, broad categories: emotions suggesting approach (positive emotions), and emotions suggesting avoidance (negative emotions). And remember to use them like so: Use emotionally implicative words (trigger words) triggering positive emotions in association with the actions you want your audience to approach, and use trigger words creating negative emotions in association with the actions you want your audience to avoid.

HOW TO INFLUENCE WITH ASSOCIATION PSYCHOLOGY

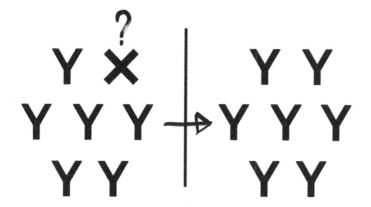

FIGURE 20: When we see a new item clumped with items of a particular kind, we tend to assume that it too is one of those items. This is influence by mere association. Present the proximity between what you argue against and patently bad items, and association psychology will blend the two together. Present the proximity between what you argue for and patently good items, and association psychology will blend the two together.

The latter produces an effect of suggesting the elimination of a source of pain (and thus more pleasure); the former produces the effect of suggesting the direct attainment of pleasure. Use both. People only move if they have pain to escape and pleasure to reach; and they move especially quickly if they are going from pain to pleasure.

If you reread this passage, you'll see how Eisenhower applies these principles to his trigger words. They aren't scattered words creating random emotional associations, they are strategic and precise, chosen for specific effect, and layered over each other in rapid sequence to reinforce that emotional effect. And no matter their nuance, all trigger words either trigger avoidance or approach.

SECRET #9:

How to use the little-known principle of broad-sweeping "mood-shifts" to empower mass movements of persuaded people.

This one is closely tied to emotion. In *All Things Shining*, authors Hubert Dreyfus and Sean Dorrance Kelly argue that a great deal of psychological meaning (and thus emotional pleasure signaling approach behaviors) can be drawn from getting wrapped up in public moods: sweeping emotional forces drawing people into a vortex of agape wonder in the face of their sheer awesomeness. Public moods are shared experiences of joy.

Public moods can be bad too. The authors caution us to identify the harmless, positive, moral and meaningful ones, the ones producing pleasure and positive meaning. And they suggest that we allow ourselves to get wrapped up in them as long as they last.

Eisenhower's use of the spectrum of the sacred and the profane matched with his use of emotionally triggering words create an overwhelming mood; a mood these young soldiers (based on countless accounts) surrendered to. This was the right choice in this case, of course. This mood would serve to alleviate a great deal of pain without producing any additional evil, giving them a sense of meaning in the face of death, destruction, and suffering. This mood was a compelling coping mechanism for the prospect of fighting a modern war, where death could come at any instant, and moments of the psychological release of relaxed safety were few and far between.

Use these principles. Try to create an overwhelming mood. The persuasive punch is unstoppable. If you see a crowd leaping to their feet at the exact same moment during a political rally, shaking the earth with their roaring applause, that's a mood.

VISUALIZING THE PRINCIPLE OF MOOD SHIFTS

OUT OF MANY, ONE

FIGURE 21: Under the spell of a public mood, the crowd becomes one, united by the moment. Persuading one is persuading all. Out of many individuals emerges one united whole, acting as a sort of meta-individual.

If you see a group of young American paratroopers (the guys who attacked Nazi Germany by jumping out of planes) singing a particular tune depicting a parachute failure and the resulting gore in a humorous light, that's a mood. And it is a mood of staring death straight in the face, unflinching. It is a mood of the highest value in this situation. It is a mood stemming from a military ethos shaped, in part, by language like Eisenhower's. Strip away the superficial elements of this situation. See the universally applicable principles defining it. Use them yourself.

SECRET #10:

How to unlock the unparalleled persuasive power of a future-based cause.

This secret dominates every single message we hack. And I didn't even try to make that happen. I couldn't find a speech that didn't apply this secret. Nobody records or remembers those speeches and messages. They aren't memorable or compelling.

I heard this principle described as vision-projecting, pacing and leading, and countless other phrases suggesting essentially the same sentiment. But when I read serial entrepreneur Russell Brunson's *Expert Secrets*, I came across the phrase "future-based cause," and I knew it captured the essence of this strategy better than any of the other phrases I've heard before.

So, what's a future-based cause? In a single sentence, a future-based cause is a cause centered on creating a better future. People don't act in the name of anything other than a future-based cause. And you can't persuade people to act if you don't invite them to chase a future-based cause, with you acting as the leader, guiding them on this chase.

It's everywhere. It's so fundamental, it's almost as fundamental as the word "the." No future-based cause? No positive persuasive results. And I don't repeat any secret more than once in this book, but look for this secret (and all secrets, for that matter) in the other speeches, and you'll find it, self-evident in its obviousness.

VISUALIZING THE FUTURE-BASED CAUSE

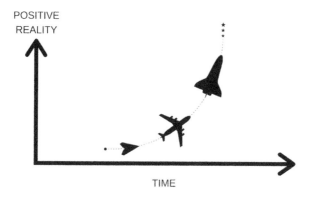

FIGURE 22: Your message must offer your audience a way to improve reality. This is foundational.

How did Eisenhower use it? "You are about to embark upon the Great Crusade, toward which we have striven these many months. The eyes of the world are upon you. The hope and prayers of liberty-loving people everywhere march with you. In company with our brave Allies and brothers-in-arms on other Fronts, *you will bring about the destruction of the German war machine, the elimination of Nazi tyranny over the oppressed peoples of Europe, and security for ourselves in a free world.*"

He described his vision for a future that would be better in three ways. This marvelous future would feature a *Destroyed German War Machine*, an *Eliminated Nazi Tyranny Over the Oppressed Peoples of Europe*, and a *Security For Ourselves in a Free World;* three benefits sorely missing from their present state.

SECRET #11:

How to avoid the biggest pitfall that will destroy all persuasive attempts no matter what else you do.

The biggest pitfall that will destroy all your persuasive attempts no matter what else you do right is forgetting to introduce the stakes (and hopefully the high stakes) of your subject matter.

Did you feel somewhat compelled by the heading of this secret? Did it make you want to read on? Now, this isn't full-proof, but chances are that yes, it did. It captivated your attention. And it did this because it introduced high stakes; because I told you it will destroy all persuasive attempts no matter what else you do.

HOW TO AVOID THE BIGGEST PERSUASIVE MISTAKE

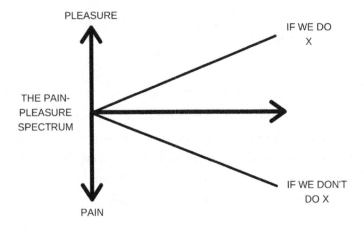

FIGURE 23: You must present stakes. If you do not present stakes, people won't be interested.

First, Eisenhower raised the stakes by referencing the amount of effort his audience already devoted to this future-based cause: "...toward which we have *striven these many months.*"

Second, Eisenhower raised the stakes by calling attention to the fact that everyone else's attention was on them. Everyone is watching you. Everyone (even the enemy, at this point) is holding their breath in anticipation. *"The eyes of the world are upon you."*

Third, and closely tied to the previous strategy, Eisenhower raised the stakes by calling attention not only to the spotlight resting on their endeavor, but on the fact that literally everyone everywhere (except for Germany, Italy, and Japan, of course) is rooting for them: "The *hope* and *prayers* of *liberty-loving people* everywhere *march* with you."

Fourth, and as an extension of the future-based cause, Eisenhower raised the stakes by letting the inherent gravity of the elements of this future based cause shine in the light of their own seriousness.

Did you observe the overlap between these strategies and the ones used to convey a sense of the sacred? This is because the sacred and high stakes are closely tied. Where you find one, the other is likely close by.

KEY INSIGHT:

We Stand at an Eternal Crossroad Between Good and Evil; the Path Up and the Path Down.

Great Speakers Artfully Remind Audiences of This, Along with Its Corollary: Everything Matters.

SECRET #12:

How to easily inspire people to act how you want them to by invoking a little-known logical fallacy.

Where there's a common logical fallacy, there's an intrinsic, inalienable, inherent and evolutionarily-ingrained feature of human psychology to use as your persuasive asset.

Fallacies are enumerated once they are observed repeatedly plaguing human judgement over a massive length of time. And if you can predict how human judgement responds to certain conditions, you can reverse-engineer the pattern to suit your persuasive goals (or more accurately, you can arrange your message to suit the pattern)

REVERSE-ENGINEERING THE PSYCHOLOGY OF FALLACIES

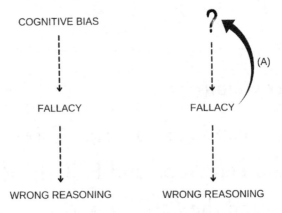

FIGURE 24: Cognitive biases create logical fallacies that lead to wrong reasoning. If you know a fallacy, you can work backward to illuminate a potential cognitive bias.

In this case, we are reverse-engineering the sunk cost fallacy: our tendency to pump resources into a sub-optimal path we invested in.

VISUALIZING THE SUNK-COST FALLACY

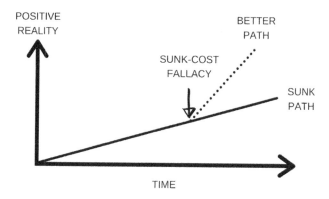

FIGURE 25: The sunk cost fallacy is continuing on a sub-optimal path simply because you sunk resources into pursuing this path in the past.

We fall victim to this fallacy for two principal reasons. First, we seek consistency (as discussed previously). Second, we feel as if we would be wasting the resources we already sunk. These two belief and behavioral patterns make us severely unlikely to give up an endeavor we sunk significant cost into.

Let's focus on how Eisenhower uses this. Let's zoom in on this sentence: "…toward which we have *striven* these *many months.*"

See how it invokes the sunk-cost fallacy? See how it references what they already gave to the cause before them? See how this makes them more likely to continue placing their energy toward the cause, even if it's going poorly? See how this, as a result, achieves Eisenhower's persuasive mission?

SECRET #13:

How to achieve instant influence and persuasive power by using the values-beliefs-policies triad.

We can broadly categorize people's sentiments into three buckets.

Bucket one: values. Values come from cultural evolution and myriad other forces acting in exceedingly complex ways. Values are our basic, fundamental, seemingly self-evident and self-validating sentiments about what is true and good regarding the essence of what it means to be human.

Values are the big-picture preferred virtues that we esteem above all else. Remember the Cold War? Remember how the United States and the Soviet Union nearly started a nuclear war, almost wiping out nearly all of humanity (or at the very least a big chunk of humanity)? The reason why was their contrary value systems. Have you ever had a romantic relationship with someone with a completely contrary value system? How did that work out? A business relationship? How did that venture end up? Why do these interactions often turn, no pun intended, nuclear? Because we see our values as fundamental truths beyond reason – that is, truths so true they don't need reasons to justify their intrinsic truth and goodness – and we therefore find it impossible to interact productively with someone operating from a completely contrary value-framework, given that our behaviors are drawn from our value-frameworks. They are axiomatic.

An example of a value is that all men are created equal, and have inalienable rights that come not from government but from our creator. Imagine having a political discussion with someone who holds the opposite sentiment as their fundamental value.

Freedom, opportunity, education, capitalism, free speech, equal opportunity, community, sacrifice, democracy, individual rights, and constitutionalism are American values. Our most extreme, vicious, and vitriolic arguments are those around values. When someone doesn't share our values, we can't interact with them in productive, peaceful, ordered ways. We have such drastically different ends in mind that we can never agree on the means.

Bucket two: beliefs. Values are big statements about what is good and true regarding the most important questions of human existence. Beliefs stem from values. Beliefs are basic statements about what should happen. They are our general, often unsubstantiated assumptions about the world, how it works, and why things happen. This includes what should happen. Beliefs change in two ways: first, little by little, chipped at over time, or second, in the sweeping after-effects of a tragic or traumatic event. They are essentially ethical assertions. And values create beliefs.

Do you have the value that all men are created equal and have inalienable, God-given rights? A belief stemming from this value could be the belief that the government should not infringe upon our freedom of speech, an inalienable right enshrined in your value. People with the same values can, on fringe occasions, develop different beliefs.

Beliefs are formed largely through socialization. The values of a culture are indoctrinated in the youth from birth. Like values, beliefs can change slowly, little by little, or in fast sweeps after shocking events. Values are set in significantly harder stone than beliefs.

Bucket three: policies. A policy is a thought about how society should go about manifesting a belief. Policies are statements of "who should do what." If your belief is that a free press is a positive thing, a policy could be guaranteeing all news outlets space to operate in the White House, for example. We have most of our disagreements over policies. Policy debates are some of the most respectful and civil arguments. Debates about beliefs? Those get stormier. Debates about values? Those are downright catastrophic. The big, huge political divide everyone is talking about these days? It's division over values, which is why it's so persistent and severe. Yes, America disagrees on beliefs and policies, but those disagreements stem from a schism in the realm of values.

The outcome of all communication hinges on the psychology of the mind that receives it, the aggregate mental characteristics of the audience members, and how the speaker's communication interacts with those two things.

So, how are values, beliefs, and policies related? How do these three categories of sentiments interact? In short: Values create beliefs, and beliefs create policies.

The value of freedom creates the belief that a free market is inherently just because it allows for voluntary transactions between free agents, which creates the policy of "Congress should deregulate the financial industry," and probably thousands of others.

Nobody disagrees with values. It's hard to imagine people arguing against freedom and getting anywhere with it. People can disagree with beliefs because while beliefs are derived from values, they can often fork in different directions. For example, two people can be both vehemently in support of freedom (who wouldn't be?), while one believes that a free market is just because it guarantees freedom, and another believes that a command economy is just because free markets can create inequality and inequality can degrade freedom.

We covered how they interact with each other. How do you interact with them? Never, under any circumstances, at any time, argue against the values of your audience members. Channel them. Make your proposals seem like they both support the values and manifest the values; that they guarantee the longevity of the values and spring forth from the values. "We believe in [insert policy] because we value [insert value]. This policy manifests [insert value] because [insert reasons]. This policy protects [insert value] because [insert reason]. This value is the foundation of [insert policy] because [insert reasons]."

HOW TO INTERACT WITH THE VALUES OF THE AUDIENCE

FIGURE 26: Your proposals must both channel the values and perpetuate the values. The values must inform the creation of your proposal (or seem to), and your proposal must seem to ensure the values are not breached.

Eisenhower invokes the values of his audience members. "You are about to embark upon the Great Crusade, toward which we have striven these many months. The eyes of the world are upon you. The hope and prayers of *liberty (value one: liberty)* loving people everywhere march with you. In company with our *brave (value two: courage)* Allies and brothers-in-arms on other Fronts, you will bring about the destruction of the German war machine, the *elimination of Nazi tyranny (value three: the defeat of a regime built around a contrary value system)* over the oppressed peoples of Europe *(value four: healing and protecting the victims)*, and security *(value five: security)* for ourselves in a *free (value six: freedom)* world."

SECRET #14:

How to recognize coded persuasive imagery in communication.

Eisenhower appropriately codes religious imagery into his communication.

"You are about to embark upon the *Great Crusade*, toward which we have striven these many months. The eyes of the world are upon you. The hope and *prayers* of liberty-loving people everywhere march with you.

It produces a powerful impact. It draws religious listeners into the message with a layer of personal meaning. And it still carries sacred associations that create impact for the non-religious as well.

PASSAGE #3:

Your task will not be an easy one. Your enemy is well trained, well equipped and battle-hardened. He will fight savagely.

SECRET #15:

How to always draw people into a captivating and compelling persuasive narrative.

Got no problem? You've got a big problem...

If your persuasive communication doesn't outline a problem, but simply dwells on a solution without discussing the problem it solves, it lacks impact.

What you want people to do is medicine. Don't talk about the medicine without talking about the sickness it solves. Sickness validates the need for the medicine; the problem validates the need for the solution.

Presenting a problem – which is an absolute prerequisite of influence – also creates room for sneaking in plenty of emotionally-triggering (avoidance-activating) implicative language, and the problem itself creates a strong avoidance motivation; a strong impulse to "move away," and to do so toward your solution.

Above all, remember this: Persuasion is speaking to get people to move, and people only move toward pleasure or away from pain. The most motivating and persuasive scenario is moving away from pain and toward pleasure. The problem supplies the pain, the solution supplies the pleasure, and people can't resist making the leap from pain to pleasure when you use this structure correctly.

In this passage, Eisenhower presented what would be a big problem for anyone going to war (or participating in any high-stakes competition): Your opponent is damn good.

But he doesn't just leave it there (as you'll see). Doing so isn't persuasive and isn't moving. It's paralyzing. Instead, he presents the problem as part of the structure revealed in the next secret.

PROBLEMS VALIDATE SOLUTIONS

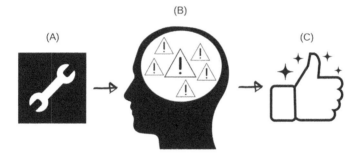

FIGURE 28: Trying to sell a solution (A) when to the audience it appears as if the reality of the world is shouting "DANGER, PROBLEM, FIX IT, DANGER, PROBLEM, FIX IT; PAIN, FAILURE, STRUGGLE, DESPERATION" (B) is more likely to result in success (C).

KEY INSIGHT:

The Strongest Impetus to Truth Is Facing the Consequences of Deceit.

WHAT HAPPENS IF YOU DON'T PRESENT A PROBLEM?

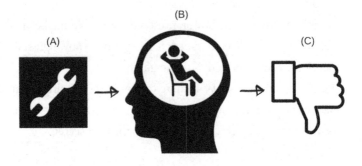

FIGURE 27: Trying to sell a solution (A) when to the audience it appears as if the reality of the world is telling them to "relax" (B) is more likely to result in failure (C).

KEY INSIGHT:

Don't Let the Brutal Truth of a Tough Situation Go Unnoticed. Help It Barge Through the Door.

The Motive for Acting Is Solving a Problem. Denying the Problem Denies the Need for Good Action

---

SECRET #16:

How to boil down all persuasion to a simple, proven, three-step structure capable of convincing anyone to do anything.

A structure formed by three simple steps creates a massive persuasive punch. It's called the "PAS" structure: problem, agitate, solution.

First, describe a problem ("Your task will not be an easy one."). Second, emotionally agitate the problem ("Your enemy is well trained, well equipped and battle-hardened. He will fight savagely.") Third, present a solution to the problem, creating massive pleasure, relief, and motivation to act.

If you only learn one thing from this book, let it be this structure. It's simple and versatile, capable of producing a tremendous amount of influence very quickly.

There are four key principles of structures. Think of them as the four laws of structure.

VISUALIZING THE FOUR LAWS OF STRUCTURE

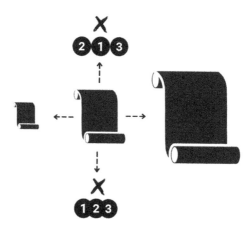

FIGURE 29: You can shorten a structure and it will maintain a proportional impact. You can lengthen it and it will maintain a proportional impact. You must follow the steps in their exact order. You must not overlap the steps.

First, the law of expansion. You can stretch the structure out like an accordion and it maintains the same impact on a different scale, as long as all the steps maintain their proportion relative to the whole.

Second, the law of reduction. You can deliver these stories in ten minutes, five minutes, or thirty seconds. Again: If you maintain proportion, the impact retains its inherent quality and persuasive strength. This makes the stories (and all structures) extremely versatile: You can stretch or shorten them to fit any possible timeframe and need.

Third, the law of precise tracing. You must precisely trace the structure. This is key. Don't entrust yourself to this structure and deviate from it unnecessarily. The steps are sequenced for a reason. Trust them. Follow them. Use precise tracing. Don't screw around with the structure. It is what it is because it is proven to work; because time and time again, it has produced the desired result. I have seen this structure repeated time and time again in countless speeches by people who, in the process, produced immense persuasive impact, and have succeeded because of it. Omit nothing, and include nothing that is not in the structure by default (unless you understand the more advanced principles of structure). Take the structure from beginning to end in a straight line, and do not get wrapped up in tangents and parentheticals. Think of a communication structure as a road, specifically designed to get you from point A to point B. In this case, point A is little persuasion, and point B is a superabundance of persuasion. And it's not just any road, but a narrow bridge, 1,000 feet over white-water rapids down below. It's a thin road. It's easy to deviate from it. There are no barriers stopping you from driving right off it. And it's windy up there on the bridge. Follow the road. The white-water rapids below represent the failed communication that occurs when you stop following the structure. If you decide to use a structure, commit to it. If you decide to get on the bridge, stay on it until the end.

Fourth, the law of separation of concerns. Don't try to accomplish step five in step one. A structure is a sequence of steps. The sequence generates the persuasive strength. And if you don't separate out the steps distinctly, blurring the lines between steps, perhaps by sticking step five anywhere except between steps four and six, you lose the persuasive strength.

SECRET #17:

How to captivate immediate attention from everyone with this simple, straightforward strategy.

Now, Eisenhower didn't only speak to the strength of the enemy for rhetorical effect. He said it because it was the right thing to do. He said it because it was true.

Thus, we arrive at the strategy of radical truth telling, of divulging the brutal truth.

People are sick and tired of language designed to obscure, minimize, or distract. People have had it with politicians and those in positions of power reneging on their moral mandate and then lying about it. People are finished with hearing anything but the truth, the full truth, and nothing but the truth, no matter how brutal a particular truth might seem to the one who has to say it.

So, what does this mean? If you give people the brutal truth, in a spirit of total transparency and complete honesty, you will control their attention, earn their trust, and become drastically more persuasive because the brutal truth supplies a problem for the PAS structure.

This is truer today than it was when Eisenhower showed us how to divulge the brutal truth to control attention. To put it bluntly, "your enemy is extremely well-trained, well-equipped with state-of-the-art killing machines, and devoted to his twisted cause," isn't a pretty picture. And weaker leaders might try to keep the people happy and minimize, mitigate, or draw attention away from the brutal truth. Ignorance is bliss, right? Wrong. Ignorance isn't bliss. Or, it only is until the world starts falling apart around you, at which point your blissful ignorance is replaced by the most painful, surprising sense of fear and betrayal.

Legendary leaders tell people the things that are hard to tell people, but that they need to hear. Legendary leaders divulge the brutal truth, and therefore control undivided attention. Hearing a leader today divulging the brutal truth is a breath of fresh air, isn't it? So, be that leader. Call out the elephant in the room. Talk about the uncomfortable but necessary reality. Challenge the familiar beliefs. Expose the impending threat.

And let me present the rule of minimization-reciprocation. Do not obscure the brutal truth, or you will be obscured. Do not mitigate the brutal truth, or you will be mitigated. Do not minimize the brutal truth, or you will be minimized.

Divulge the brutal truth, no matter how hard it is to say and how hard it is to hear, no matter how comfortable ignorance might be, and no matter how tempting it might be to beat around the bush. Adopt a spirit of honesty and transparency at all times, and as a leader, you shall be rewarded with honor and total respect. Not to mention that you will control complete attention, and achieve massive persuasive impact.

PASSAGE #4:

But this is the year 1944! Much has happened since the Nazi triumphs of 1940-41. The United Nations have inflicted upon the Germans great defeats, in open battle, man-to-man. Our air offensive has seriously reduced their strength in the air and their capacity to wage war on the ground. Our Home Fronts have given us an overwhelming superiority in weapons and munitions of war, and placed at our disposal great reserves of trained fighting men. The tide has turned! The free men of the world are marching together to Victory!

SECRET #18:

How to wrap up the most compelling persuasive structure ever discovered.

In this passage, Eisenhower explains the solution. There are two ways to do this: Why is the problem either no longer a problem (a more inspirational, empowering tack) or what can they do to solve it (a more motivating tack)?

He opted for the first. It made sense in his persuasive context. Inspiration is a brand of persuasion dedicated to making people believe they can do something, or making people do something they would do anyway with a more empowered and productive mindset.

The structure of presenting a problem and offering a solution works, in part, because of the contrast effect. Using the contrast effect is presenting differences between your subject and another item to enhance, diminish, emphasize, or deemphasize an aspect of your subject. The contrast effect appeals to comparative perception: forming beliefs based on differences between a subject of evaluation and a point of comparison.

The meanings of two opposite (or contrasting) words seem more extreme placed together. The sound of a trombone seems deeper followed by a high-pitched trumpet. White seems brighter next to black, and black darker next to white. When you perceive two contrasting items simultaneously, their contrasting qualities are emphasized.

HOW THE CONTRAST EFFECT PREVENTS CONFUSION

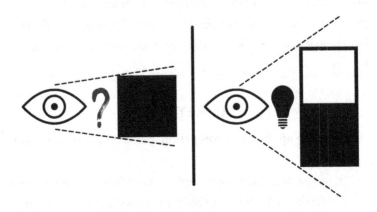

FIGURE 30: Humans perceive the world and make judgements by comparing things. In the absence of any available comparison, people miss the point and get confused. No comparison, no judgement. No judgement, no influence. The point of camouflage is to reduce contrast. Don't camouflage your point, rendering it invisible against its background. Do the opposite. Create contrast.

One particularly compelling example of the contrast effect in action? Real estate salesmen use it to get higher offers for the same homes. Watch out for this if you're buying a house soon. They'll show you three homes. Home one is run-down, ugly, and overpriced at $500,000. Home two is also run-down, ugly, and overpriced at around $500,000. Home three? Beautiful, perfect, completely sound, and competitively priced at the phenomenal, once-in-a-lifetime price of $400,000.

What's going on here? They artificially inflated the asking price of homes one and two, while maintaining or just slightly raising the asking price of home three. Home three is the only one priced at market value. Due to the contrast effect, buyers perceive home three as much nicer and significantly more well-priced than homes one and two. Why? Because they compare and contrast the three deals. They don't judge the third item in isolation, but stack it against the preceding two. The result? An instantaneous purchase of home three.

Why does this work? What is the hidden secret of human perception, decision-making, and judgement at work here, putting irresistible and instantaneous influence in your reach? Comparative perception: Humans cannot judge the value of an item in a vacuum; they need points of reference, relativity between two or more items, and ways to compare the salient item to points of reference.

In short: Because the prospects perceive two unattractive offers prior to the moderate offer, it suddenly appears outstanding. Why? Because the buyer contrasted it to the two unattractive offers. If the contrasts didn't influence them – if the agent just showed them home three – they probably would be less excited about it. Why? Because there would be no artificial points of comparison making it seem phenomenally well-built and well-priced.

HOW THE CONTRAST EFFECT SHAPES YOUR REALITY

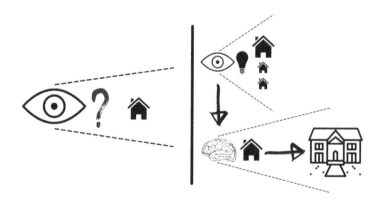

FIGURE 31: If real estate agents show a customer a house in isolation, the contrast effect is not in play. The customer does not instinctively leap to a particular conclusion as a result of interpreting contrasts. However, by pre-framing the same house with two worse offers, the real estate

agents activate the contrast effect, altering the prospect's reality by giving him an outsized impression of the better house.

Let's quickly talk about the science behind the contrast effect before getting into the critical questions: How can you use it in communication? How can you use it to ethically persuade with ease? How can you make people reflexively gravitate towards you, your message, and your ideas?

17th century philosopher and polymath John Locke first observed the contrast effect in its purest form: Stick your hand in hot water, then put it in lukewarm water. The lukewarm water will seem cold. Now, stick your hand in icy-cold water, and put it in the same lukewarm water. It will seem hot.

The core principle? Differences between items just perceived and items currently perceived influence human perception. Let's call the $400,000 house the lukewarm water. Because buyers previously perceived two "icy-cold" offers, the lukewarm house seemed hot. It comes down to this fundamental truth of economics: Everything is a choice between alternatives. Thus, we compare alternatives to form judgements. No comparison, no judgement. This is true of colors, sounds, textures, temperatures, and most salient to you, ideas, proposals, and offers, as well as the contrasting emotional states caused by the problems and solutions.

SECRET #19:

How to apply the hidden, little-known process of emotional-sentiment-agitation.

Agitation is extremely powerful. Remember when we discussed the four rules of structure? Remember when we discussed the idea of stretching? How you could take a structure and make it 80,000 words, or deliver it in three sentences, and it would maintain the same persuasive punch with a proportional magnitude?

Agitation is simply increasing the intensity of a rhetorical effect, while stretching refers to stretching its actual length. But often, it just so happens the best way to agitate is not only swapping in more intense phrases, but simply lengthening the whole message altogether.

And you already encountered agitation: We just unpacked the Problem, *Agitate*, Solution structure. And in this passage, Eisenhower shows us how we can agitate anything. It doesn't have to be the problem step of the PAS structure. It can be the solution step of the PAS structure (creating the PASA structure). It can be any idea or sentiment presented on its own. It can be the curiosity created by your hook. You can agitate anything.

And what is the PAS structure really doing? It's creating the correct emotional states in a correct sequence; a sequence which empowers their persuasive punch. It's hijacking the 1,000,000-year-old emotional structures buried in the deepest layers of our brain and using them to create the right set of thoughts to produce the right set of actions.

Agitating simply escalates these emotional states, leading to more persuasive punch (more of the desired thoughts and, theoretically, more of the resulting actions). The structure is the same; the sequence is the same; the emotional states are the same. What changes? The strength and intensity of the emotions.

How do you agitate? There are countless ways. But what does Eisenhower do? He simply repeats, in a sort of stack, statements agitating the same core sentiment: "But this is the year 1944! Much has happened since the Nazi triumphs of 1940-41. (This implies the solution to the previously-described problem, and is the core statement he agitated). The United Nations have inflicted upon the Germans great defeats (1), in open battle (2), man-to-man (3). Our air offensive has seriously reduced their strength in the air (4) and their capacity to wage war on the ground (5). Our Home Fronts have given us an overwhelming superiority in weapons (6) and munitions (7) of war, and placed at our disposal great reserves of trained fighting men (8). The tide has turned! (9) The free men of the world are marching together to Victory! (10)"

Bringing back the idea of moods for a moment, which of the following do you think would create the most overpowering and irresistible shared mood? The core sentiment ("But this is the year 1944! Much has happened since the Nazi triumphs of 1940-41")? Or the core sentiment followed by ten agitating statements?

This type of stacked, escalating rhetorical repetition is a versatile tool in your persuasive arsenal, capable of agitating any emotion to the point of its peak persuasive effect.

KEY INSIGHT:

The Art of Rhetorical Agitation Is the Art of Turning a Mundane Fact Into an Undeniable and Unmistakable Orchestra that Rings with Truth and Power.

It Is a Rhetorical Avalanche.

SECRET #20:

How to use this common-sense (but always forgotten) strategy to make people trust you and follow your lead with enthusiasm.

Proof is the ultimate agitator.

Proof is inherently persuasive.

Proof works.

But so many people try to persuade people to follow their lead, but forget to provide supporting proof and evidence validating their proposed action.

If you analyze this passage, you'll see that all the agitators are simply pieces of supporting proof, validating the solution.

People say "emotion persuades, and people then use facts to support their emotional conclusions." This forgets a crucial relationship: Facts create emotions. All this proof creates more relief by creating more belief in the solution, and this creates more action.

SECRET #21:

How to use the limiting-belief-handling structure to help people defeat their limiting beliefs (reliably eliminating objections).

This is a structure in a structure. This is using a structure to achieve one of the steps of another structure. It is a problem, agitate, solution structure, and the solution is a limiting-belief-handling structure. This sub-structure orients part of the persuasive message around examples of the audience already having the qualities they need to have to do what they want. It makes your audience feel like they are capable. It makes the audience confident in their abilities. It builds the speaker to audience connection.

Use this when you have personal knowledge of your audience; when you recall examples of your audience expressing the necessary qualities; when you want to inspire a specific group of people to believe they can do something insurmountably difficult.

Start by presenting the limited frame: "You might think that you aren't capable of achieving [goal]." Present the goal: "Here's the specific goal you want to achieve. You might think you can't." Present the necessary qualities: "Here are the qualities you need to achieve that goal. You already have these qualities." Example one: "Here's the first time you showed me you have these qualities." Example two: "Here's the second time you showed me you have these qualities." Example three: "Here's the third time you showed me you have these qualities." Continue as needed.

VISUALIZING THE CORE PRINCIPLE OF INSPIRATION

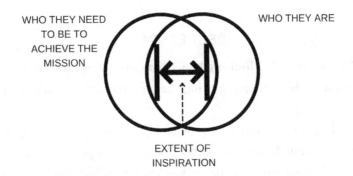

FIGURE 32: The core of inspiration is presenting the overlap between who they need to be and who they are.

Eisenhower followed the exact steps implicitly if not explicitly.

This structure says, "you have everything you need to do what you want to do." You are taking a goal your audience thought was unreachable, and putting it within reach by showing them extremely specific examples proving that they already have exactly what it takes.

It systematically removes limiting beliefs, empowering your audience to believe they can do what you are trying to persuade them to do.

PASSAGE #5:

I have full confidence in your courage, devotion to duty and skill in battle. We will accept nothing less than full Victory!

SECRET #22:

How to make a simple two-letter change to instantly make your audience subconsciously feel like you are on their team.

Pay attention to this: "I have full confidence in your courage, devotion to duty and skill in battle. *We* will accept nothing less than full Victory!"

"We" is a magic word. It is an inclusive pronoun, and carries a dramatically effective persuasive punch. It makes your audience feel included in your message, like you are a team member striving with them for the common goal, and like you have empathy for them, their struggles, and their desires.

Simply changing words like "you" and "yours" to "we" and "ours" can completely reverse the sentiment of a message, making it significantly more persuasive by including the audience in the message, and casting the speaker as the spokesperson for the team.

As we can see, Eisenhower used inclusive pronouns in other passages too: "But this is the year 1944! Much has happened since the Nazi triumphs of 1940-41. The United Nations have inflicted upon the Germans great defeats, in open battle, man-to-man. *Our* air offensive has seriously reduced their strength in the air and their capacity to wage war on the ground. *Our* Home Fronts have given us an overwhelming superiority in weapons and munitions of war, and placed at *our* disposal great reserves of trained fighting men. The tide has turned! The free men of the world are marching together to Victory!"

That's deliberate intent, not an accident.

Compare that to this: "But this is the year 1944! Much has happened since the Nazi triumphs of 1940-41. The United Nations have inflicted upon the Germans great defeats, in open battle, man-to-man. *The* air offensive has seriously reduced their strength in the air and their capacity to wage war on the ground. *The* Home Fronts have given us an overwhelming superiority in weapons and munitions of war, and placed at *the disposal of this army* great reserves of trained fighting men. The tide has turned! The free men of the world are marching together to Victory!"

SECRET #23:

How to master the one sentence persuasion course for instant influence in any situation.

In *The One Sentence Persuasion Course*, Blair Warren argues that you can "make the world do your bidding" by persuading people with five core strategies: encouraging their dreams, allaying their fears, justifying their failures, throwing stones at their enemies, and confirming their suspicions.

In this closing sentence, Eisenhower applies some of this wisdom from Blair Warren: "I have full confidence in your courage, devotion to duty and skill in battle." He allays their fear of defeat by saying, "We will accept nothing less than full victory!"

The core emotional apparatus of approach and avoidance doesn't just apply to ideas and potential actions. It applies to people. And if our emotional sensors are suggesting approach toward a person, we are significantly more likely to feel the same about the ideas they share and the proposals they present. This is why "be liked by your audience" is such an effective persuasive strategy.

Think about the function of allaying people's fears: Your presence itself becomes associated with the pleasure of escaping the pain of fear. Their emotions are "approach, approach, approach." And that extends beyond you, to the ideas you share.

Throughout Eisenhower's speech, other examples of this simple five-part framework saturates the language. He threw stones at their enemies quite a bit, for example, with the language about eliminating the German war machine, and all the examples of the Allied Expeditionary Force inflicting defeats on the German armies.

THE FIVE STRATEGIES FOR IRRESISTIBLE INFLUENCE

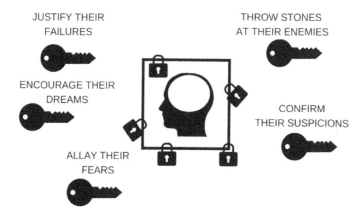

FIGURE 33: People "will do anything" (according to Blair Warren) for those who justify their failures, encourage their dreams, allay their fears, throw stones at their enemies, and confirm their suspicions. These are the five keys that will unlock cognitive defenses.

SECRET #24:

How to use expectation-projection to quickly make people feel irresistibly pulled to act a certain way.

This strategy channels a force of similar nature to that of psychological self-identity. Give people an expectation or reputation to live up to, and they will. Something like, "Hey, I heard from so many people that you're really helpful and know your stuff, so would you mind helping me with...?" can usually do the trick in most interpersonal situations. The person will think, "Yes! I am that way (invoking self-identity)! I want to prove this person right!" They will then act accordingly.

This same exact dynamic occurred when Eisenhower said, "I have full confidence in your courage, devotion to duty and skill in battle." He gave them a reputation to live up to; this reputation implied a positive expectation, and they lived up to it, displaying extra courage, extra devotion, and extra skill.

SECRET #25:

How to use the little-known principle of belief transfer to hijack mirror neurons for your persuasive benefit.

We have neurons in our brains that simulate an emotional "mirror" of the actions we see. It's why we can learn complex physical skills by watching an expert do it: Our mirror neurons activate, simulate the skill, and embed the information in our minds. So, in part of making the shift from you to them, focus intently on their facial expressions. Your automatic mirror neurons will mirror the physical action you see (a tiny, fast, and involuntary facial muscle shift that would escape your conscious mind) and simulate it, creating the same feeling the facial shift betrayed in the person. Thus, you'll get a window into their emotional state.

This is why presenting an emotional message calls for wearing the emotion on your face. When people see the facial expression, mirror neurons cause them to experience the emotion behind it themselves. And a similar process occurs with our processing of language. Sad language can make us sad. Happy language can make us happy. We adopt the emotions of the characters we observe.

REVEALING THE NEUROBIOLOGY OF EMPATHY

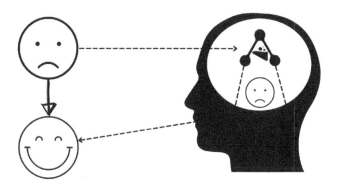

FIGURE 34: When you perceive, for example, an unhappy facial expression, mirror neurons simulate the feeling associated with the expression, revealing to you that it is an unhappy expression. As a result, you can observe the negative state of the audience, and provide the message you think will "turn that frown upside down."

This is the remarkable neurobiology behind the scenes in this passage, and the same reason why countless legendary leaders make statements like, "I have full confidence in your courage, devotion to duty and skill in battle. We will accept nothing less than full Victory!"

These statements portray the leader's personal confidence in the outcome of the cause; a belief which transfers into the minds of the audience, making them feel more confident in themselves, and thus more likely to take action, follow through, and succeed.

PASSAGE #6:

Good luck! And let us beseech the blessing of Almighty God upon this great and noble undertaking.

.........................Chapter Summary.................................

- The fundamental persuasive structure is the "problem-solution" structure. This is the ground of all persuasion.
- The structure can be expanded and built upon. For example, you can add an "agitate" step after the problem.
- Powerful words and persuasive narratives appeal to the psychology of the minds receiving the communication.
- For example, psychological identity, the group instinct, the primacy effect, the consistency principle, and many others.
- To motivate action, you must rally people behind a future-based cause. The action must bring about a better future.
- The higher the stakes of your message, the more impact and influence it carries, all else equal.

KEY INSIGHT:

Your Empathy Is Your Superpower. To See Through the Eyes of Your Audience Members, to Know Their Pain & Promise, Their Fears & Dreams, Is to Connect On the Deepest Level.

YOUR PERSUASIVE TOOLBOX (PART ONE)

1	Use Eisenhower's Rhetorical Secrets
1.1	Appeal to Psychological Self-Identity
1.2	Form a Psychological Coalition
1.3	Activate the Primacy Effect
1.4	Use the Principle of Persuasive Consistency
1.5	Present Contextual Pre-framing
1.6	Call Out Your Audience by Their Salient Identity
1.7	Apply the Sacred-Profane Spectrum
1.8	Use Aristotle's 2,000-Year-Old Persuasive Key
1.9	Instigate Broad-Based Emotional "Mood Shifts"
1.10	Present a Future-Based Cause
1.11	Remember to Introduce High Stakes
1.12	Reverse-Engineer the Sunk-Cost Fallacy
1.13	Apply the Values, Beliefs, Policies Triad
1.14	Recognize and Use Connotative Coded Imagery
1.15	Justify Your Persuasive Narrative by Confronting a Problem
1.16	Apply the Problem, Agitate, Solution Structure
1.17	Divulge the Brutal Truth
1.18	Wrap Up the Foundational Structure with Contrast
1.19	Apply Emotional-Sentiment-Agitation Aimed at the Solution

1.20	Use Proof as an Emotional Agitator
1.21	Present the Limiting-Belief-Defusing Structure
1.22	Replace "You" and "I" with "We"
1.23	Implement the Five Parts of the One-Sentence Persuasion Course
1.24	Apply Expectation-Projection
1.25	Use the Principle of Belief-Transfer
2	**Use Clinton's Rhetorical Secrets**
3	**Use Reagan's Rhetorical Secrets**

Email Peter D. Andrei, the author of the Speak for Success collection and the President of Speak Truth Well LLC directly.

pandreibusiness@gmail.com

KEY INSIGHT:

We Are Wired to Feel Deep Compassion Toward People, Not Abstractions; Toward Stories, Not Statistics.

THREE WAYS... TWO WRONG, ONE RIGHT

DON'T PRETEND IT'S EASY (NAIVE OPTIMISM)

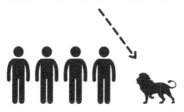

DON'T PRETEND IT'S HOPELESS (CYNICYSM)

TELL THE TRUTH, AND THEN INSPIRE

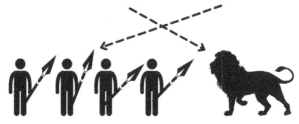

Claim These Free Resources that Will Help You Unleash the Power of Your Words and Speak with Confidence. Visit www.speakforsuccesshub.com/toolkit for Access.

18 Free PDF Resources

12 Iron Rules for Captivating Story, 21 Speeches that Changed the World, 341-Point Influence Checklist, 143 Persuasive Cognitive Biases, 17 Ways to Think On Your Feet, 18 Lies About Speaking Well, 137 Deadly Logical Fallacies, 12 Iron Rules For Captivating Slides, 371 Words that Persuade, 63 Truths of Speaking Well, 27 Laws of Empathy, 21 Secrets of Legendary Speeches, 19 Scripts that Persuade, 12 Iron Rules For Captivating Speech, 33 Laws of Charisma, 11 Influence Formulas, 219-Point Speech-Writing Checklist, 21 Eloquence Formulas

Claim These Free Resources that Will Help You Unleash the Power of Your Words and Speak with Confidence. Visit www.speakforsuccesshub.com/toolkit for Access.

30 Free Video Lessons

We'll send you one free video lesson every day for 30 days, written and recorded by Peter D. Andrei. Days 1-10 cover authenticity, the prerequisite to confidence and persuasive power. Days 11-20 cover building self-belief and defeating communication anxiety. Days 21-30 cover how to speak with impact and influence, ensuring your words change minds instead of falling flat. Authenticity, self-belief, and impact – this course helps you master three components of confidence, turning even the most high-stakes presentations from obstacles into opportunities.

Claim These Free Resources that Will Help You Unleash the Power of Your Words and Speak with Confidence. Visit www.speakforsuccesshub.com/toolkit for Access.

2 Free Workbooks

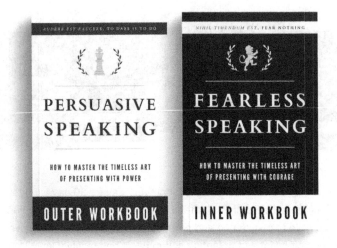

We'll send you two free workbooks, including long-lost excerpts by Dale Carnegie, the mega-bestselling author of *How to Win Friends and Influence People* (5,000,000 copies sold). *Fearless Speaking* guides you in the proven principles of mastering your inner game as a speaker. *Persuasive Speaking* guides you in the time-tested tactics of mastering your outer game by maximizing the power of your words. All of these resources complement the Speak for Success collection.

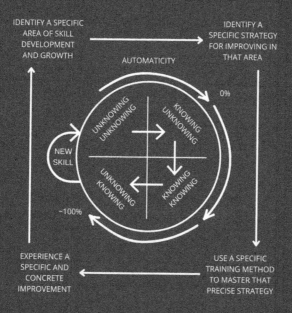

How do anxious speakers turn into articulate masters of the craft? Here's how: With the bulletproof, scientifically-proven, 2,500-year-old (but mostly forgotten) process pictured above.

First, we identify a specific area of improvement. Perhaps your body language weakens your connection with the audience. At this point, you experience "unknowing unknowing." You don't know you don't know the strategy you will soon learn for improving in this area.

Second, we choose a specific strategy for improving in this area. Perhaps we choose "open gestures," a type of gesturing that draws the audience in and holds attention.

At this point, you experience "knowing unknowing." You know you don't know the strategy. Your automaticity, or how automatically you perform the strategy when speaking, is 0%.

Third, we choose a specific drill or training method to help you practice open gestures. Perhaps you give practice speeches and perform the gestures. At this point, you experience "knowing knowing." You know you know the strategy.

And through practice, you formed a weak habit, so your automaticity is somewhere between 0% and 100%.

Fourth, you continue practicing the technique. You shift into "unknowing knowing." You forgot you use this type of gesture, because it became a matter of automatic habit. Your automaticity is 100%.

And just like that, you've experienced a significant and concrete improvement. You've left behind a weakness in communication and gained a strength. Forever. Every time you speak, you use this type of gesture, and you do it without even thinking about it. This alone can make the difference between a successful and unsuccessful speech.

Now repeat. Master a new skill. Create a new habit. Improve in a new area. How else could we improve your body language? What about the structure of your communication? Your persuasive strategy? Your debate skill? Your vocal modulation? With this process, people gain measurable and significant improvements in as little as one hour. Imagine if you stuck with it over time. This is the path to mastery. This is the path to unleashing the power of your words.

Access your 18 free PDF resources, 30 free video lessons, and 2 free workbooks from this link: www.speakforsuccesshub.com/toolkit

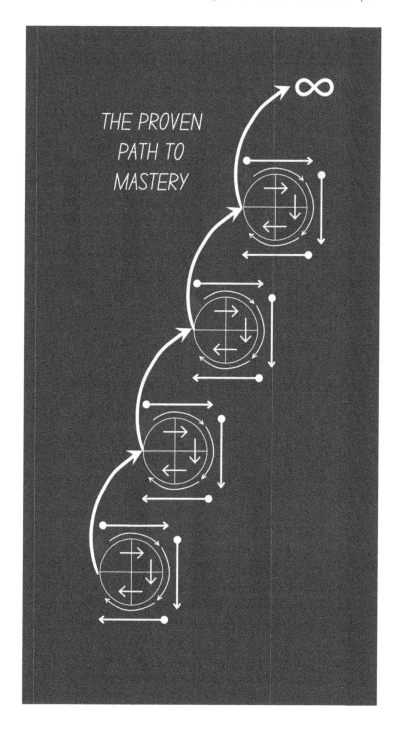

SPEAK FOR SUCCESS COLLECTION BOOK

XIII

THE LANGUAGE OF LEADERSHIP CHAPTER

III

DURING REBIRTH:

Bill Clinton's First Inaugural Address

"TODAY WE CELEBRATE THE MYSTERY OF AMERICAN RENEWAL…"

B ILL CLINTON ENTERED OFFICE IN A TIME OF challenge and opportunity. The United States was suffering, struggling under the crushing weight of a mountain of challenges; grasping for forward strides while stuck in the mire of stagnation; struggling to keep its head above water in the wake of a disastrous recession.

Imagine saving for decades, striving to improve your economic standing, and finally purchasing an idyllic home for your family only to be rudely awoken from your American dream by the stunning realization you have to lose it all and start from scratch.

Millions of Americans lost their homes, their jobs, their livelihoods; families struggled to provide their kids the life all children deserve.

And in the darkness of this mounting disaster, Clinton knew every word had to count. He knew every word had to repair the broken American spirit. He knew every word had to inspire confidence. He knew every word had to contribute something to the mission of persuading people to place their faith in him, in themselves, and in their country.

A new world of technology, globalism, and free trade rose from the ashes of the old, and America struggled to find its identity in this new world. After testing countless means of conducting national life, seemingly switching with every new administration, America struggled to find a firm set of principles upon which to launch its adventure into this new world. Clinton also knew he needed to persuade people to adopt the right principles for success in an unprecedented age.

What did he say? What deeply compelling persuasive strategies did he use to repair America and set it on a sequence to ever-higher successes in an unfamiliar world? Let's find out.

PASSAGE #1:

My fellow citizens: Today we celebrate the mystery of American renewal.

SECRET #26:

How to command attention from the very beginning and set the stage for successful persuasion.

If you don't start your communication with a "hook," you might as well not start at all. On a fundamental psychological level, hooks appeal to the key algorithm governing human decisions. "Giving this person attention" is a decision.

The algorithm is as follows: "If the benefit of this action (for example, receiving this message and listening intently) exceeds the costs (the mental calories spent paying attention), and is the most beneficial action available, then I'll do it."

REVEALING HOW PEOPLE DECIDE WHAT TO DO

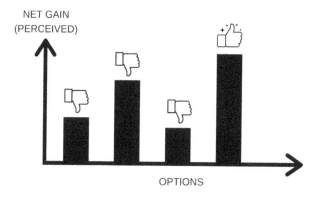

FIGURE 35: If an option has the highest perceived net gain of all the other options available, people select that option. Thus, a major sub-goal of your persuasive effort is to raise the perception of net gain associated with your proposal.

And in about eight seconds after you start speaking, people run through the algorithm, and make their decision. So, if you don't hook them in those first eight seconds, you've lost before you've even really began.

But how do you formulate a hook? There are countless strategies, mountains of different approaches, and vast numbers of "best practices." But I prefer sticking to one tried-and-true, time-tested, proven, and infallible method. Arouse curiosity. Doesn't the mystery of American renewal grab your attention?

PASSAGE #2:

This ceremony is held in the depth of winter. But, by the words we speak and the faces we show the world, we force the spring. A spring reborn in the world's oldest democracy, that brings forth the vision and courage to reinvent America.

SECRET #27:

How to guarantee people follow your lead by offering a paradigm shift.

Want people to actually get excited about your ideas? Want people to talk about them, spreading the word for you? Want people to actually follow through instead of forgetting about your proposal? Then don't offer them a better version of an old idea. Offer them a paradigm shift.

Henry Ford, the creator of the first consumer car, said that if he asked people what they wanted, they would have said faster horses. Faster horses are a better version of an old idea, not a paradigm shift. Cars were a paradigm shift; an entirely new opportunity; something so inventive they took over transportation, redefined American life, and made Ford rich.

VISUALIZING A NEW PARADIGM VERSUS INCREMENTALISM

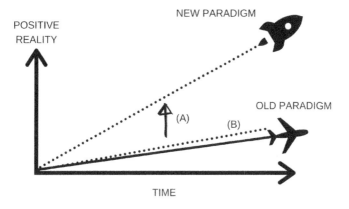

FIGURE 36: A paradigm shift jumps to an entirely new mode of achieving the desired results (A) rather than offering a slightly better version of the same thing (B).

The vision Clinton offers the American people is not an improved America. It's a reinvented America. It's a reborn America. It's a new America in a new world, not a marginally better version of the old one. Apply the same principle to your offers, proposals, and ideas, and people will receive them with drastically more enthusiasm.

PASSAGE #3:

When our founders boldly declared America's independence to the world and our purposes to the Almighty, they knew that America, to endure, would have to change. Not change for change's sake, but change to preserve America's ideals; life, liberty, the pursuit of happiness. Though we march to the music of our time, our mission is timeless. Each generation of Americans must define what it means to be an American.

SECRET #28:

How to use ideal-invocations to create an immediate pull toward the action you propose.

Why do so many speakers like Clinton use the phrase "life, liberty, the pursuit of happiness?" It goes beyond the obvious. They do it because these three ideals are fundamental values everyone seeks to manifest in the world. They do it because centuries of American life centered around these ideals. They do it because people are socialized from an early age to prize these values above all else.

Clinton creates a compelling persuasive pull by playing on ideals he knows are both worthy and inherently hammered into people's heads as values worth protecting.

PASSAGE #4:

On behalf of our nation, I salute my predecessor, President Bush, for his half-century of service to America. And I thank the millions of men and women whose steadfastness and sacrifice triumphed over depression, fascism and communism.

SECRET #29:

How to throw stones at people's enemies to subtly bring them into your orbit of influence.

Remember *The One Sentence Persuasion Course.* Remember how you can achieve a shockingly influential presence by throwing stones at people's enemies. This is exactly what Clinton does here: "And I thank the millions of men and women whose steadfastness and sacrifice triumphed over depression, fascism and communism"

PASSAGE #5:

Today, a generation raised in the shadows of the Cold War assumes new responsibilities in a world warmed by the sunshine of freedom but threatened still by ancient hatreds and new plagues.

SECRET #30:

How to use alternating semantic-sentiments to captivate people and compel action.

Contrast is everything in persuasion. We talked about that already. But now, we're going to discuss a particularly compelling method of captivating people's attention and motivating action that builds upon the elements of contrast we discussed previously.

Rapidly alternate between positive sentiment and negative sentiment. It's an unstoppably effective method of psychological persuasion because it appeals to innate characteristics of human cognition, like perception through comparison (we make judgements based on comparing things, never considering them in isolation), emotion-oriented attention (we direct our attention to whatever arouses our emotions), and anti-habituation (that which forms a predictable pattern "habituates" and loses our attention because we believe we've figured it out). This method provides plenty of contrast, plenty of emotional arousal, and plenty of anti-habituation by alternating between opposite sentiments.

How did Clinton do this? "Today, a generation raised in the shadows of the Cold War (-) assumes new responsibilities in a world warmed by the sunshine of freedom (+) but threatened still by ancient hatreds and new plagues (-)."

You don't know what to think or how to feel, but you're not confused about it either. It keeps you on your toes without overwhelming you. It's brilliantly effective for drawing people in, a key element of persuasion because all persuasive endeavors are accomplished in two steps: persuading them to listen to your persuasive message, and delivering the message itself. This strategy accomplishes the first step.

PASSAGE #6:

Raised in unrivaled prosperity, we inherit an economy that is still the world's strongest, but is weakened by business failures, stagnant wages, increasing inequality, and deep divisions among our people.

SECRET #31:

How to connect two separate paradigms with alternating semantic sentiments to build an influential narrative.

Persuasion demands influential narratives. You need to build a story, organizing the complex world into a relatively simple pattern of existence suggesting your proposed action as the best path forward.

Narratives demand unity. There has to be some semblance of constancy in a narrative. Rapidly jumping from one segment to a totally different segment without a clear unifying element loses people. It's confusing. You momentarily lose confused people, and when you momentarily lose people, you raise the perceived cost of the communication beyond the perceived gain. The goodwill you built at the start with your hook is lost until you permanently lose them.

Before technological advances in firefighting, people would stand in a line connecting a water source to the fire, passing buckets of water from person to person. This was called a bucket brigade. You want your message to pass people's attention from segment to segment just like a bucket brigade smoothly passes the water from person to person. And don't spill the attention, or else the building might burn down.

And people intuitively understand stories and narratives, and that which we find intuitive is also more influential to us. This is known as the intuitive bias, which is a meta-cognitive bias; a cognitive bias made out of other cognitive biases.

So, what exactly is this strategy? It's none other than semantic sentiment alternation as we discussed previously, but continued over a shift in subject matter. It's continuing the alternation of sentiment from the previous segment (a segment discussing a different subject than the current one), thus acting as a unifying element. "Today, a generation raised in the shadows of the Cold War (-) assumes new responsibilities in a world warmed by the sunshine of freedom (+) but threatened still by ancient hatreds and new plagues (-) *[section one, talking about America's foreign affairs, ends, and section two, talking about America's domestic affairs, begins]* Raised in unrivaled prosperity, we inherit an economy that is still the world's strongest (+), but is weakened by business failures, stagnant wages, increasing inequality, and deep divisions among our people (-)."

PASSAGE #7:

When George Washington first took the oath I have just sworn to uphold, news traveled slowly across the land by horseback and across the ocean by boat. Now, the sights and sounds of this ceremony are broadcast instantaneously to billions around the world.

SECRET #32:

How to use a then-and-now construction to emphasize the need for novelty.

We discussed how people are dramatically more attracted to new things rather than mere improvements on the old ones. We talked about the persuasive power of paradigm shifts. This strategy builds upon that.

A then-and-now construction is exactly what it sounds like. First, describe what happened then: "When George Washington first took the oath I have just sworn to uphold, news traveled slowly across the land by horseback and across the ocean by boat." Second, describe what's happening now: "Now, the sights and sounds of this ceremony are broadcast instantaneously to billions around the world."

Of course, the then and the now phases have to be thematically united. In this case, the unifying idea was the speed of communication. Why does it work? And how does it build upon paradigm shifts? Using the then-and-now emphasizes the drastic difference between the past and the present, thereby validating the need for a new paradigm as opposed to a better version of the old paradigm.

KEY INSIGHT:

Put the Present into the Context of History. Show Them Where This Moment Came From.

Then, Show Them How They Can Chart An Upward Course Into Tomorrow.

PASSAGE #8:

Communications and commerce are global; investment is mobile; technology is almost magical; and ambition for a better life is now universal. We earn our livelihood in peaceful competition with people all across the earth.

SECRET #33:

How to instantly rouse people to action by sharing the opportunities of the moment.

Evolution ingrained in us archetypal understandings of the world around us: concepts we intuitively understood preverbally (that is, before the evolution of language).

THE DEEPLY INTUITIVE NATURE OF ARCHETYPES

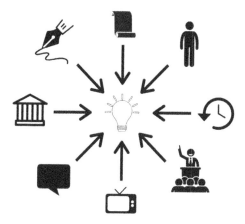

FIGURE 37: Archetypes are essential basic patterns that reoccur across different art forms, forms of communication, times, places, and cultures. They are embedded deep in the collective unconscious and offer you massive intuitive appeal if you know how to use them.

These ideas are broad and basic, centering on active interactions with the world: the threat, the predator, the prey, the danger, the challenge, the opportunity.

This kind of language – language describing opportunities like "investment is mobile; technology is almost magical" – connotes the following sentiment: "We, right now, are sitting in front of myriad opportunities like we've never had before, and these offer us everything we could possibly need to survive and thrive."

The human mind, with its archetypal, preverbal understanding of the idea of an opportunity (something that might help us survive and thrive), supplies the natural follow-up: "Wow – we really are sitting on opportunities. What better time to get moving? Let's act now." Remember this: An idea you got your audience to form themselves is infinitely more persuasive than one you hammered in there yourself.

Present an opportunity. Coded in people's genes (but not infallibly – sometimes other forces are more prevalent), is the tendency to direct attention to and act on opportunities. And getting people to act is the essence of persuasion and leadership.

PASSAGE #9:

Profound and powerful forces are shaking and remaking our world, and the urgent question of our time is whether we can make change our friend and not our enemy.

SECRET #34:

How to present a moment of decision to always command attention and inspire enthusiastic action.

Decisions demand attention. An impending moment of decision, for which one is yet undecided, creates a tension like none other. Think about the moments in your own life, when you know you need to decide something, but you can't bring yourself to do it just yet. Doesn't that impending decision, that fork in the road, seem to always creep into your consciousness, no matter how hard you try to suppress it?

Why does Clinton say what he says in this passage? Because he understands that moments of decision loom large in people's consciousness and that when they are faced with an impending moment of decision, they direct their attention subconsciously and automatically toward anything that might help them make the decision. And that is the key to this strategy. People subconsciously and automatically direct their attention to anything related to the decision. Your communication is related to the decision in a major way. See how this simple strategy can control a tremendous amount of attention (a precondition for persuasion) with little effort?

PASSAGE #10:

This new world has already enriched the lives of millions of Americans who are able to compete and win in it. But when most people are working harder for less; when others cannot work at all; when the cost of health care devastates families and threatens to bankrupt many of our enterprises, great and small; when fear of crime robs law-abiding citizens of their freedom; and when millions of poor children cannot even imagine the lives we are calling them to lead, we have not made change our friend.

SECRET #35:

How to create cognitive dissonance and portray pain to easily leverage a massive persuasive push.

You know people strive to attain pleasure and escape pain. And you know if you want to inspire and persuade people to take an action, you sometimes need to draw attention to a problem they have, hitting their pain-points over and over again.

Cognitive dissonance is the psychological pain we feel when we sense a contradiction between what we believe about reality and reality. For example, when we know we should act a certain way and clearly see we aren't, cognitive dissonance kicks in.

And in this passage and the previous one, Clinton essentially said this: "We must make change our friend. We haven't made change our friend."

What internal mental monologue does the audience have in this moment? "We must make change our friend. (They accept this belief about how they should act). We haven't. (They feel the pain of cognitive dissonance as they realize a contradiction between what they believe they should do and what they've done)."

What is the persuasive payoff of creating this cognitive dissonance? What is the point of illuminating problems in the first place? To validate your solution; to make people feel a deep need for whatever can solve the problem. It's the same principle here. By kicking up cognitive dissonance, Clinton created a need to achieve resolution; a need to escape the tension; a need to hear what he has to say next which, presumably, would provide that resolution.

PASSAGE #11:

We know we have to face hard truths and take strong steps. But we have not done so. Instead, we have drifted, and that drifting has eroded our resources, fractured our economy, and shaken our confidence.

SECRET #36:

How to use a want-got gap to immediately make people feel ethically compelled to do what you want.

The persuasive structure of this passage is a want-got gap: structuring a persuasive message around presenting a gap between what people want and what they have, and then inspiring them to close the gap.

It uses the aspirations of the audience as persuasive fuel. It creates cognitive dissonance. It justifies the inspiration and empowerment in the context of the gap.

Use it when your audience has a clear gap in their lives they could fill; when you want to inspire your audience; when you want to empower them to close the "want-got" gap.

Present the want: "Here's what you want to have in your life." Present what they have: "Instead, here's what you actually have. It's not what you want." Create repetitive want-got contrast: repeatedly jump back and forth, contrasting what they want with what they have. Provide empowerment: "But you can get what you want. You have what it takes to bridge the gap." Present an action for closing the gap: "The first step is..."

VISUALIZING THE POWER OF THE WANT-GOT STRUCTURE

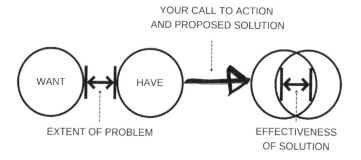

FIGURE 38· A problem is a gap between what they want and what they have (or an overlap between what they don't

want and what they have). Your call to action and proposed
solution promise to increase the "want" and "got" overlap.

A common mistake speakers make when trying to inspire is only doing the empowerment. But the empowerment becomes a lot more powerful in the context of a want-got gap.

PASSAGE #12:

Though our challenges are fearsome, so are our strengths. And Americans have ever been a restless, questing, hopeful people. We must bring to our task today the vision and will of those who came before us.

SECRET #37:

How to call people to action by presenting their duty of carrying on a long-lasting legacy.

People feel countless cultural pressures – we typically call them social pressures – to act certain ways. You can tap into their psychological need to not let people down, stemming from their psychological need for approval from the "tribe."

Present a legacy of the group to which they belong, a legacy of acting how you want them to act (or thinking how you want them to think). They will subconsciously want to avoid disappointing their "tribe" at large, whatever that might mean, and feel compelled to carry on a legacy – a legacy of doing exactly what you want them to.

Clinton wants his audience to feel strong; to feel restless in their pursuit of progress; to be a questing, hopeful people. And he makes clear that this is a bigger cultural legacy and not a list of random ideals with this critical sentence: "We must bring to our task today the vision and will of those who came before us."

The subtle psychological implication is that they must carry on the legacy. "Don't let us down. Everyone is watching."

And recall the consistency principle. This strategy is to individual consistency appeals what group psychological identity is to individual psychological identity. This strategy appeals to the need for consistency not with one's prior actions but with the prior actions of the associations and groups supporting one's group identity.

KEY INSIGHT:

Group Identity Is a Double-Edged Sword, the Sword of Tradition and of Tyranny.

Use It to Empower People, Convey Truth, and Strengthen Your Audience's Noble Instincts.

PASSAGE #13:

From our revolution, the Civil War, to the Great Depression to the civil rights movement, our people have always mustered the determination to construct from these crises the pillars of our history.

SECRET #38:

How to use a micro-limiting-belief-handling construction to get people to believe in you, your cause, and themselves (in one sentence).

We talked about the limiting-belief-handling structure. This is a micro-structure following along similar lines. It's applying the rule of shortening. It connects the cultural pressure to carry on a legacy with an immensely subtle element of judgement: The group you represent has a legacy of acting correctly; you should be able to also, right?

Let's perform message-hacking in the purest form. Let's take the persuasive message from a legendary leader, and generalize every phrase. "From our revolution (previous example of his audience acting how he wants to persuade them to act now), the Civil War (previous but more recent example of his audience acting how he wants to persuade them to act now), to the Great Depression (previous but more recent example of his audience acting how he wants to persuade them to act now), to the civil rights movement (previous but more recent example of his audience acting how he wants to persuade them to act now), our people have always mustered the determination to construct from these crises the pillars of our history (enumeration of the positive qualities portrayed and the ideal to strive for)."

And there you have it: the generalized, abstract structure you can apply to your specific subject. This illustrates the essence of message-hacking.

PASSAGE #14:

Thomas Jefferson believed that to preserve the very foundations of our nation, we would need dramatic change from time to time. Well, my fellow citizens, this is our time. Let us embrace it.

SECRET #39:

How to appeal to human loss-aversion to create an irresistible pull into your orbit of influence.

Loss-aversion is an incredibly compelling feature of human psychology you can use to empower your persuasive efforts with ease. Simply put, humans suffer the pain of loss more than they relish the pleasure of gain, sometimes up to twice as much. As a natural extension, we fear the pain of loss more than we hope for the pleasure of gain.

REVEALING WHY LOSS HURTS MORE THAN GAIN

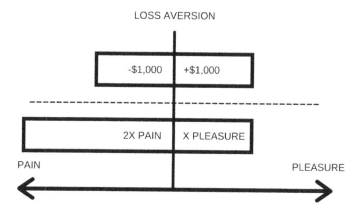

FIGURE 39: People have been shown to regularly fear loss more than they hope for an equivalent gain. While the extent of loss aversion differs between people, it can often be a factor of two.

In short: We are naturally designed to be conservative players of the game of life. Protecting ourselves from pain and the loss causing it is up to twice as psychologically attractive as striving for pleasure and the gain causing it.

As a result, we are risk-averse, preferring to protect what we have (assuming we have anything relevant to the situation at hand to begin with) rather than risking it in a chase for more. So, all in all, you can create an immensely irresistible persuasive pull by promising just that; by promising protection. Present benefits that are not just positive things to gain; present benefits in the form of guarantees against loss.

Clinton subtly, with only a few words, invoked this inherent, overpowering need to protect. "Thomas Jefferson believed that to *preserve the very foundations of our nation,* we would need dramatic change from time to time. Well, my fellow citizens, this is our time. Let us embrace it." Keyword: Preserve.

PASSAGE #15:

Our democracy must be not only the envy of the world but the engine of our own renewal. There is nothing wrong with America that cannot be cured by what is right with America.

SECRET #40:

How to promise means to make your plans, proposals, and ideas believable (thus significantly more persuasive).

There is a debate among persuasive writers: Is it better to talk about the features of a product, or its benefits? This is aimed at the algorithm governing human action and raising perceived benefit to balance the equation in your favor.

Benefits are the positive outcomes your audience will experience as a result of listening to you or taking your suggested action. Features are what create the benefits. What about your suggested action will produce those benefits? Those are the features. When you want to speak in terms of self-interest and tip the algorithmic equation in your favor, what do you use? Benefits, or features?

This is a deeply divisive question in marketing and advertising. What sells more, the benefits of a product, or the features that produce those benefits? And in reference to persuasive communication, what appeals to people's self-interest more? What makes perceived reward higher? Benefits, or features?

Speaking in terms of only features is the worst, and speaking in terms of only benefits is okay. Luckily for you, you don't have to pick one. It's a false dilemma. Speak in terms of both features and benefits. Describe a feature and then explain the benefits of that feature, or start with benefits and explain the features that create them.

Remember, ideas are products that people need to "buy."

This is what features-only sounds like: "This healthcare plan will decentralize the planning of aggregate treatments, and instead use blockchain and feedback infrastructure to determine what treatments to enact and when to enact them." *What does that soup of big complicated words even mean? I have no idea what this politician is trying to say. Can't he just tell me how this will impact my life? I really don't trust him anymore, and I have no faith in this healthcare plan because I don't know what it means for my life.*

This is what benefits-only sounds like: "This healthcare plan will make you pay less money and receive better treatment." *Woah! That sounds great. I see how that will impact my life. I definitely would love to pay less money. That's a huge plus. And I need better treatment. But it's just a promise. Can I trust it? It sounds good, but will it really happen? I'm doubting this. I'm intrigued, but not fully on-board.*

This is what features and benefits sound like: "This healthcare plan will decentralize the planning of aggregate treatments, and instead use blockchain and feedback infrastructure to determine what treatments to enact and when to enact them, which will make the whole system less wasteful and more efficient, and therefore make you pay less money and receive better treatment." *I'm blown away! I definitely would love to pay less money and receive better treatment. This is perfect. And what a well-thought-out plan! It makes perfect sense. I know exactly how this will impact my life, and exactly how it's going to work. I trust this guy and his plan. I'm going to donate to his campaign and vote for him!*

When you're promising benefits to someone, they want to believe you. But without explaining the features that create those benefits, they often can't. And if your features are particularly complex, throw in a bridge statement to connect your features to your benefits in a believable and understandable way.

Think of benefits as answering the question, "what does this action give me that I want?" while features answer the question "how does this action give me what I want?" Features empower the benefits, making them believable.

THE RELATIONSHIP BETWEEN THE "WHAT?" AND "HOW?"

HOW CREDIBLE PLANS SUPPORT COMPELLING BENEFITS

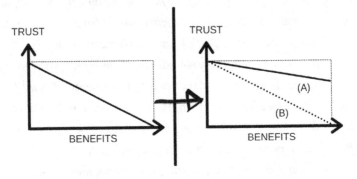

FIGURE 40: As benefits rise, in many cases, trust begins to fall. It sounds too good to be true. However, when you have a credible plan, this relationship weakens (A) as opposed to when you lack a credible plan (B).

What does this passage accomplish? It presents means; features creating the benefits; a plan which, even in its abstract nature, lends the benefits credibility by explaining how they can be manifested:

"what is right with America (feature)," and "our Democracy (feature)" can be the "engine of our own renewal."

PASSAGE #16:

And so today, we pledge an end to the era of deadlock and drift; a new season of American renewal has begun. To renew America, we must be bold. We must do what no generation has had to do before. We must invest more in our own people, in their jobs, in their future, and at the same time cut our massive debt. And we must do so in a world in which we must compete for every opportunity. It will not be easy; it will require sacrifice. But it can be done, and done fairly, not choosing sacrifice for its own sake, but for our own sake. We must provide for our nation the way a family provides for its children.

SECRET #41:

How to get people thrilled to follow through on your ideas by promising benefits and answering the "WIIFM?" question.

You know that people go through a fundamental psychological algorithm in their heads when they decide if they should act. You also know they do this constantly, always scanning for changes that might upset the original balance between benefits and costs first initiating an action. What you don't know is that you should particularly focus on satisfying this mental algorithm in two places: the first eight seconds with a hook (as we discussed), and when you call them to action. So, how can you do this, no matter where you need to do it? Promise benefits. Answer the critical question everyone is asking themselves constantly: "what's in it for me?"

Tell them how their lives can become better, just like Clinton did: "We must invest more in our own people, in their jobs, in their future, and at the same time cut our massive debt."

I want to emphasize what we discussed in the previous section: Combining benefits and features produces the most persuasive impact. But speak more about benefits than features. They are significantly more compelling.

PASSAGE #17:

Our Founders saw themselves in the light of posterity. We can do no less. Anyone who has ever watched a child's eyes wander into sleep knows what posterity is. Posterity is the world to come; the world for whom we hold our ideals, from whom we have borrowed our planet, and to whom we bear sacred responsibility. We must do what America does best: offer more opportunity to all and demand responsibility from all.

SECRET #42:

How to dive deep to the hidden reasons to do what you want, reveal them, and get massive opt-in with irresistible psychological appeal.

People have a pyramid of human desires. We desire X. Why do we desire X? Because it satisfies desire Y; and Y satisfies desire Z; and Z satisfies desire J, so on and so forth until we hit the desires that are inherently desired, and not sought because they satisfy some other desire.

At the top of this pyramid are the most fundamental, widely shared, and powerful desires; we can even argue the other desires below them on the pyramid are all just manifestations of these few fundamental desires on the top.

So, how do you dive deep into human psychology and leap up the pyramid to drive at the core motivating factors that can instigate enthusiastic action? With the manifold-why algorithm. First, identify the benefits you offer your audience attached to your action that build persuasive value. Second, pick one (you'll do it for all of them if needed). Third, ask yourself these questions: "Why is this good? Why do they want it?" Fourth, answer the questions: "They want it because it... (you jumped a level up on the pyramid now, identifying the desire the first desire satisfied)." Fifth, repeat this. Each answer will bring you a layer up the pyramid, closer to the core, fundamental desires connected to your initial benefit; the ones producing the most persuasive punch. Sixth, stop when you either can only answer "I don't know why we want it – we just do," or the answer isn't because it satisfies another desire.

In the previous section, Clinton appealed to some desires lower on the pyramid: a job, better education, and the like. People want these. And people don't only want them, they desperately need them. So, they are deeply compelling.

But it's best to match them with these top-of-pyramid desires. And that's exactly what Clinton did: "Our Founders saw themselves in the light of posterity. We can do no less. Anyone who has ever watched a child's eyes wander into sleep knows what posterity is. Posterity is the world to come; the world for whom we hold our ideals, from whom we have borrowed our planet, and to whom we bear sacred responsibility."

What top-of-pyramid desire did he promise to satisfy, and thus invoke as a benefit? The desire to see our children succeed.

It's brilliant. He hits at a core feature of the evolution of human psychology: inclusive fitness. In evolutionary terms, "fit" members of a species have a high chance of passing on their genetic material. Inclusive fitness is the desire to protect those who share our genetic material: our children (and our siblings, etc.) People who had the desire to see their DNA live on in their children protected their children; and those who didn't have this desire didn't protect their children to the same degree. Thus, over time, everyone developed this desire to protect their children (because the desire is a massively beneficial adaptation increasing the likelihood of survival for the children who carry forward the genetic lineage containing the trait).

WHAT DO MOST PEOPLE WANT?

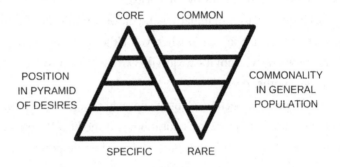

FIGURE 41: The core desires are more common, and any particular specific desire is less common. The closer you are to core desires – the higher the level of abstraction at which you define a desire – the more common it is.

THE PYRAMID OF HUMAN DESIRES

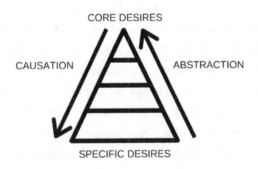

FIGURE 42: Specific desires at the bottom of the pyramid are particular manifestations of core desires; particular

ways of achieving the core desires. Core desires cause desires which cause desires which cause desires *ad infinitum*, but are not themselves caused by any other desire. The level of abstraction rises as you move up the pyramid. It is narrower at the top because there is a small handful of core desires, but a virtually infinite number of specific manifestations of these core desires.

I just imagine him asking himself, "Now, beyond the obvious, why do people want a better job? A better education? More economic opportunity?" Aha! That's it. For their kids and their kid's kids..."

KEY INSIGHT:

Some Moral Principles, Some Human Truths, Some Worldly Aims, Are Not Valued for the Sake of Other Principles, Truths, or Aims, But for Their Own Inherent Worth.

Do Not Build Your Message on a Foundation of Sand, But on a Firm Bed of Moral Granite.

PASSAGE #18:

It is time to break the bad habit of expecting something for nothing, from our government or from each other. Let us all take more responsibility, not only for ourselves and our families but for our communities and our country. To renew America, we must revitalize our democracy.

SECRET #43:

How to use the frame presentation-escalation strategy to appear clairvoyant and sophisticated.

This is a ubiquitous strategy in the words of legendary leaders. Instead of only saying, "Let us all take more responsibility, not only for ourselves and our families but for our communities and our country (what we should do)," they precede this by saying, "It is time to break the bad habit of expecting something for nothing, from our government or from each other (what we shouldn't do)."

It presents the incorrect frame and escalates from this frame to a superior one. It uses the power of persuasive contrasts, establishing not only what someone stands for, but what someone stands in opposition to, ultimately creating a more vivid sense of the cause at large. In short: With this type of structure, the second statement – the escalated frame – sounds more compelling in the context of the first frame.

The investing course marketing manager could apply it like so: Instead of only saying "It's time to take control of your finances and sow the seeds for financial freedom," they could first say "It's time to stop undermining your future by continuing dozens of poor financial habits that empty your bank account. It's time to take control of your finances and sow the seeds for financial freedom." See how the first empowers the second? See the power of the contrast effect? See how this is another kind of pre-framing?

PASSAGE #19:

This beautiful capital, like every capital since the dawn of civilization, is often a place of intrigue and calculation. Powerful people maneuver for position and worry endlessly about who is in and who is out, who is up and who is down, forgetting those people whose toil and sweat sends us here and pays our way.

SECRET #44:

How to gain automatic authority and earn instant trust by revealing a hidden conspiracy.

People trust the person who levels with them and tells them the truth. And people let those they trust persuade them, because they don't fear getting tricked into taking a loss. Moreover, if you recall from *The One Sentence Persuasion Course*, people are persuaded by those who confirm their suspicions.

And those are the simple principles behind the persuasive power of this passage. Clinton is illuminating the hidden truth about what really goes on in Washington. But crucially, people already largely suspect it. So, he earns trust by illuminating a "conspiracy," but also by confirming what they already largely suspected. (While throwing stones at their enemies, of course).

Remember: Subtle, implicative persuasion works. People have a conscious mental filter and it loves to question flat-out persuasive appeals presented in a forceful, bland manner. These subtle statements sneak right under the filter and bury themselves in the mind, where they slowly turn people over to your way of thinking.

There is a subtle statement through implication made when Clinton reveals the conspiracy and confirms their suspicions about the hidden truth. It casts him as different from those wrapped up in the conspiracy he's illuminating, thus presenting him as someone worth following. Saying "there are people over there doing bad things" implies "I am not one of them." But could you say "I am not one of the people doing bad things" flatly? Of course not. You cannot present some meanings directly. You must imply them gently and subtly.

PASSAGE #20:

Americans deserve better, and in this city today, there are people who want to do better. And so I say to all of us here, let us resolve to reform our politics, so that power and privilege no longer shout down the voice of the people. Let us put aside personal advantage so that we can feel the pain and see the promise of America. Let us resolve to make our government a place for what Franklin Roosevelt called 'bold, persistent experimentation,' a government for our tomorrows, not our yesterdays. Let us give this capital back to the people to whom it belongs.

SECRET #45:

How to speak to broken justice problems to make your proposal irresistible.

In *Building a Storybrand*, Donald Miller discusses story-selling and the problem-solution structures it inherently calls for. And in this context, he presents the three different types of problems: external, internal, and moral.

External problems exist in the outside world. For example, low sales performance exists externally. Internal problems exist within someone. External problems create internal problems. For example, low sales performance creates the internal problem of anxiety and insecurity at work. Lastly, moral problems wrap up the external and internal problems in a unified moral narrative, explaining why it's wrong, and revealing why the internal and external problems are flat-out immoral and unjust. They are problems of injustice, not petty inconveniences.

So, which should you use? All of them.

External problems are strong because of their specificity; because they point to tangible, real-world deficiencies. Internal problems are strong because of their emotional resonance; because they call out problematic emotions associated with the external problem. Don't forget this key point: External problems and internal problems are linked. External problems cause internal problems. Where do moral problems come in? They explain how the external problems and the internal problems represent more than just an inconvenience or disappointment, but a fundamental moral wrong.

Moral problems outline how the combination of external and internal problems represent a deep breach of fairness, not just a little, forgettable problem. This makes the entire problem-solution structure significantly more persuasive, and drastically more likely to inspire action. Moral problems outline how the victim of the external and internal problems doesn't deserve to deal with them.

How does Clinton use these principles to achieve massively compelling persuasive impact? "Americans *deserve* better *(no, they don't want better, they deserve better: it's a moral imperative),* and in this city today, there are people who want to do better. And so I say to all of us here, let us resolve to reform our politics, so that power and privilege no longer shout down the voice of the people. Let us *put aside personal advantage* so that *we can feel the pain* and see the promise of America. Let us resolve to make our government a place for what Franklin Roosevelt called 'bold, persistent experimentation,' a government for our tomorrows, not our yesterdays. *Let us give this capital back to the people to whom it belongs.* "

And from this emerges a sophisticated structure, wrapping up many of the preceding insights. Layer the victim-perpetrator-benevolence triad over the problem-agitate-solution structure while presenting the three kinds of problems.

First, explain why they are victims of an external problem with internal and most importantly moral ramifications (problem, three kinds of problems, victim). Second, explain who the perpetrator is. Who is to blame? Who is victimizing them? Here's how it links to the first step to form a unified and compelling narrative: How did the perpetrator create the external problem, setting off the internal problem and the moral breach? This functions as the agitate step (agitate, perpetrator). Third, portray your personal benevolence, and how you're going to protect the victims from the pain, defeat and punish the perpetrator, and restore justice to the world (solution, benevolence).

The structure is P3V, AP, SB: Present the three kinds of problems victimizing them, agitate the problems by presenting the causal perpetrator, and present your benevolent solution.

Let us identify the structure in this passage. It's possible he stretched the structure here and there. He didn't actually have the step-by-step framework we do. We're looking for the key points in roughly the correct order.

"This beautiful capital, like every capital since the dawn of civilization, is often a place of intrigue and calculation. Powerful people (enumeration of perpetrator) maneuver for position and worry endlessly about who is in and who is out, who is up and who is down, forgetting those people whose toil and sweat sends us here and pays our way (external problem)."

"Americans (victims) deserve better (moral problem), and in this city today, there are people (benevolence) who want to do better (solution). And so I say to all of us here (benevolence), let us resolve to reform our politics (solution), so that power and privilege (perpetrator) no longer (solution) shout down the voice of the people (moral problem). Let us put aside personal advantage so that we can feel the pain (internal problem) and see the promise of America (benevolence). Let us resolve to make our government a place for what Franklin Roosevelt called "bold, persistent experimentation (solution)," a government for our tomorrows, not our yesterdays. Let us give this capital back to the people to whom it belongs (benevolence)."

In short: This structure combines the PAS structure with a triad of characters; the victim (the audience), the perpetrator (the person or group that caused the external problem and the associated pain), and the benevolent source of good (the speaker, who will protect the victims from the perpetrator, throw stones at the perpetrator, replace pain with pleasure for the victim, and fix the moral problem). It also breaks down rhetorical problems into the external, internal, and moral categories, using them to paint a moral narrative about why the audience must act and why the source of benevolence is worth following.

The core of this structure is shockingly ubiquitous in the language of the 2020 Democratic primary candidates, leading me to believe they realized Clinton was the most persuasive leader the party has had for decades.

Bernie Sanders: "Well, Judy, what I would say is that we have a president who is a pathological liar (perpetrator). We have a president who is running the most corrupt administration in the modern history of this country (perpetrator). And we have a president who is a fraud, because during his campaign he told working people (victims) one thing, and he ended up doing something else (perpetrator). I believe, and I will personally be doing this in the coming weeks and months (speaker as benevolent force for good), is making the case that we have a president (perpetrator) who has sold out the working families of this country (victims), who wants to cut social security, Medicare, and Medicaid, after he promised he would not do that (perpetrator), and who has documentedly lied thousands of times since he is president (perpetrator)."

Joe Biden: "Well, I don't think they really do like the economy. Go back and talk to the old neighbors in the middle-class neighborhoods you grew up in (victims). The middle class is getting killed (victims). The middle class is getting crushed and the working class has no way up as a consequence of that (victims). You have, for example, farmers in the Midwest, 40 percent of them could pay, couldn't pay their bills last year (victims). You have most Americans, if they've received the bill for 400 dollars or more, they'd have to sell something or borrow the money (victims). The middle class is not, is behind the eight ball (victims). We have to make sure that they have an even shot (benevolent force for good). We have to eliminate (benevolent force for good) significant number of these god-awful tax cuts (perpetrator) that were given to the very wealthy (perpetrator). We have to invest in education (benevolent force for good). We have to invest in healthcare (benevolent force for good). We have to invest in those things that make a difference in the lives of middle-class people (victims) so they can maintain their standard of living (benevolent force for good). That's not being done, and the idea that we're growing, we're not growing. The wealthy, very wealthy are growing (perpetrators). Ordinary people are not growing (victims). They are not happy with where they are (victims), and that's why we (benevolent force for good) must change this presidency (perpetrator) now.

Tom Steyer: "Let me say that I agree with Senator Warren in much of what she says. I've been for a wealth tax for over a year (benevolent force for good). I'm (benevolent force for good) in favor of undoing all the tax breaks for rich people (perpetrators) and big corporations (perpetrators) [crosstalk] that this administration (perpetrator) has put through. And in addition, I've talked about equilibrating the taxes on passive investment income (benevolent force for good), which would allow us to cut taxes for 95% of Americans (victims) by 10%. But there's something else going on here that I think is really important, and that's this. We know Mr. Trump's (perpetrator) going to run on the economy. I built a business over 30 years from scratch (benevolent force for good). We're (benevolent force for good) going to have to take him (perpetrator) on, on the economy in terms of growth as well as economic justice (benevolent force for good). We're going to have to be able to talk about growth, prosperity across the board for everyone in America (benevolent force for good). My experience building a business, understanding how to make that happen (benevolent force for good) means I can go toe to toe with Mr. Trump (perpetrator) and take him down on the economy and expose him as a fraud and a failure. And I think that's different from the other people on this stage. I think we need a different unconventional way of attacking a different unconventional president (perpetrator) who actually went after the best prepared candidate in American history and beat her."

Elizabeth Warren: "So I see right now is, we've got to get the carbon, we've got to stop putting more carbon into the air (benevolent force for good). We've got to get the carbon out of the air and out of the water and that means that we need to keep some of our nuclear in place (benevolent force for good). I will not build more nuclear. I want to put the energy literally and the money and the resources behind clean energy and by increasing by 10-fold what we put into science, what we put into research and development (benevolent force for good). We need to do what we do best. And that is innovate our way out of this problem and be a world leader (benevolent force for good). But understand the biggest climate problem we face is the politicians in Washington (perpetrators) who keeps saying the right thing, but continue to take money from the oil industry (perpetrators). Continue to bow down to the lobbyist (perpetrators), to the lawyers (perpetrators), to the think tanks (perpetrators) to the bought and paid for experts (perpetrators). America understands that we've got to make change and we're running out of time (benevolent force for good). That climate change threatens every living thing on this planet (victims). But getting Congress to act, they just don't want to hear it (perpetrators). And if we don't attack the corruption first, if we don't attack the corruption head on, then we're not going to be able to make the changes we need to make on climate, on gun safety, on drug pricing, on all of the big problems that face us. We need a Washington that doesn't just work for the rich and the powerful (perpetrators). We need one that works for our families (victims)."

Andrew Yang: "I believe everyone on this stage (benevolent force for good) would do the right thing by DREAMers (victims) in the first hundred days. I would make it a top priority (benevolent force for good). I'm the son of immigrants myself. The fact is almost half of fortune 500 companies were started by an immigrant or children of immigrants (benevolent force for good). Immigrants make our country stronger and more dynamic (benevolent force for good). And immigrants are being scapegoated for issues they have absolutely nothing to do with (victims). If you go to the factory in Michigan, it's not wall to wall immigrants (victims). It's wall to wall robot arms and machines (perpetrators). We have to send the opposite message of this administration (perpetrators) and, as your president, I think I could send a very clear message, where if you're considering immigrating to this country and I'm the president, you would realize my son or daughter can become president of the United States (benevolent force for good). That's the opposite of the current administration (perpetrators) and that's the message I would love to send to the world (benevolent force for good)."

Pete Buttigieg: "Yes, and they should have a fast track to citizenship (benevolent force for good) because what the United States did under this president (perpetrator) to them (victims) was wrong and we have a moral obligation to make right what was broken (benevolent force for good). And on the larger issue of immigration, my understanding of this issue isn't theoretical (benevolent force for good). It's not something I formed in committee rooms in Washington. It begins with the fact that my household, my family came from abroad. My father immigrated to this country and became a U.S. Citizen. It comes from the fact that I'm the mayor of a city where neighborhoods that were left for dying (victims) are now coming back to life (benevolent force for good), largely because of the contributions mainly of Latino immigrants. And I've seen those same neighborhoods shut down (victims). Families huddling in church (victims), panicking just because of the rumor of an ICE raid (perpetrator) that does not make our country safe. Just to look into the eyes of an eight year old boy (victim) whose father was deported (victim) even though he had nothing so much as a traffic ticket against his name and try to think of something to tell that boy because I couldn't tell him what he most wanted to hear, which is just that he was going to have his dad back. How can harming that young man (victim) possibly make America safer (perpetrator)? When I am president? Based on those experiences, I will make sure that this is a country of laws and of values and that means not only ending these unspeakable frugal practices at the border (perpetrator), but finally and truly fixing the immigration system (perpetrator) that has needed, a full overhaul since the 1980s (benevolent force for good)."

PASSAGE #21:

To renew America, we must meet challenges abroad as well at home. There is no longer division between what is foreign and what is domestic; the world economy, the world environment, the world AIDS crisis, the world arms race; they affect us all.

SECRET #46:

How to activate the "illusory-truth effect" (a little-known cognitive bias) to persuade with ease and sophisticated strategy.

We tend to perceive easy-to-process and repeated statements as more truthful. It's also called the reiteration effect, the validity effect, and the truth effect, though we will call it the illusory truth effect. It closely ties to our bias for familiar information.

Lawn signs. Yes: Lawn signs. Politically unaware people still vote. Lots of them. They don't read the news, keep up with the candidates, or follow the issues, but they still fulfill their Democratic duty.

So, what do lawn signs have to do with the illusory truth effect, and persuasive communication? They make one name familiar. They make one name recognizable. And we are biased towards what we find familiar. And what do we find familiar? What we repeatedly encounter and find easy to process. Consider the design of lawn signs: They are bright, easy to read, and only display last name. They fulfill one purpose, and one purpose only: name recognition. (Thinking about it through the lens of behavioral economics, it's also social proof: "Lots of people have signs in their yards endorsing this candidate, so he must be a good one").

What is another example of the illusory truth effect? Imagine taking a test you didn't study for. You see a question you can't get a handle on. It's multiple-choice. Which answer do you select? Studies prove you'll probably select the one you recognize; the one evoking familiarity. And remember, biases are rough, good-enough heuristics working well in many instances: it's possible it seems familiar because your teacher discussed it in class. Thus, it's the correct answer, while the others he never discussed represent red-herrings.

How powerful is the illusory truth effect? Repeated exposure to a falsehood tricks even those who first picked the correct answer studies prove this. Participants in studies correctly answer a question, but after repeated exposure to the incorrect answer, pick it up anyway. With great power comes great responsibility.

THE ILLUSORY TRUTH EFFECT VISUALIZED

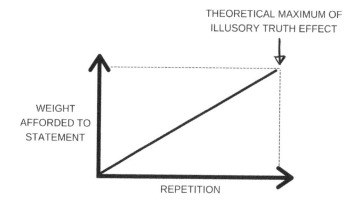

FIGURE 43: As you repeat a message, the weight afforded to the message rises.

THE SINISTER POWER OF THE ILLUSORY TRUTH EFFECT

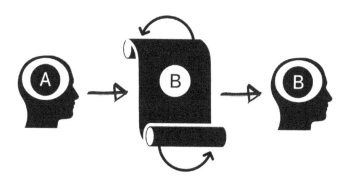

FIGURE 44: Even someone knowing the correct answer changes their response to a questionnaire when repeatedly exposed to the incorrect answer.

Different cognitive biases and mental heuristics closely tangle together in complicated webs of causation. The fluency heuristic, a form of attribute substitution, is another bias causing the illusory truth effect. We perceive information we process fluency as more truthful; we substitute the attribute heuristic "ease of processing" for "truth." Repetition raises processing ease.

"To renew America, we must meet challenges abroad as well at home. There is no longer division between what is foreign and what is domestic; the *world* economy, the *world* environment, the *world* AIDS crisis, the *world* arms race; they affect us all." By listing these world problems while repeating the word "world," Clinton activates the illusory truth effect in support of the claim that "there is no longer division between what is foreign and what is domestic," turning a millennia-old feature of human psychology, the illusory truth effect, into a persuasive asset producing irresistible psychological influence.

KEY INSIGHT:

The Repeated Claim Persists. The Persistent Claim Often Wins. Make the Repeated Claim the True One. Make It the Empowering One. Make It the Valuable One.

PASSAGE #22:

Today, as an old order passes, the new world is more free but less stable. Communism's collapse has called forth old animosities and new dangers. Clearly America must continue to lead the world we did so much to make.

SECRET #47:

How to add a single word to achieve a "tone of self-evidence" and quickly turn people to your way of thinking.

Pay attention to this word: "*Clearly* America must continue to lead the world we did so much to make."

This one single word offers a tremendous amount of persuasive value because it creates a tone of self-evidence; a tone implying the statement is obvious, self-evident, clearly true. "America must continue to lead the world we did so much to make" is a position; an opinion; an argument, up for debate. "*Clearly* America must continue to lead the world we did so much to make" is different. It's not a statement of position or opinion – it's a statement of what is self-evidently fact. Or at least that's how it's received by the minds listening to the message: as something they have to be blind not to see. Do you see the nuance?

Will this single word (or whatever phrase you use to the same effect) make the difference between a no or a yes? Opt-in or rejection of your ideas? Probably not alone. But these strategies stack. They are not used in isolation. They are each tools in your toolbox; they are each weapons in your arsenal. And you need a combined-arms approach, using them in coordination for maximum impact.

PASSAGE #23:

While America rebuilds at home, we will not shrink from the challenges, nor fail to seize the opportunities, of this new world.

Together with our friends and allies, we will work to shape change, lest it engulf us.

SECRET #48:

How to use an "or else" construction to quickly and easily get people to agree with your proposal.

Check out this last phrase: "Together with our friends and allies, *we will work to shape change, lest it engulf us.*"

Again, let us message-hack in the purest form: "...we will work to shape change (action), lest it engulf us (what happens if the action isn't taken – an "or else" statement)."

And that's the micro-structure. Remember, Clinton used it in a single sentence. You can lengthen it and shorten it at will. But, taking it at face value, here it is: propose your action, then describe the pain that not taking the action will cause.

No stakes, no story. No story, no persuasion. How can you get someone to do something? Raise the perceived benefit of doing it, raise the perceived pain of not doing it, or both. An "or else" construction accomplishes the latter.

Clinton's "or else" was abstract and vague: "...lest it engulf us." That made sense for his situation. In yours, you might want to be more specific, perhaps saying the audience might lose their biggest relevant desire or have to face their biggest relevant fear.

PASSAGE #24:

When our vital interests are challenged, or the will and conscience of the international community is defied, we will act; with peaceful diplomacy when ever possible, with force when necessary. The brave Americans serving our nation today in the Persian Gulf, in Somalia, and wherever else they stand are testament to our resolve.

SECRET #49:

How to use the ease-difficulty (and/or peace-war) duality to present yourself as a strong leader worth following.

In an anecdotal study I conducted (the evidence isn't scientifically full-proof due to sample size insufficiency), I presented about 70 people with three plans for dealing with a crisis in Syria.

The first plan was a war-monger's dream: Send in the troops. The second plan might as well have been tweeted by an angelic dove: No troops, no matter what. The third plan – the one called the "Peace First Plan" – was a mix: No troops except special forces deployed defensively to protect key human resources like Red Cross volunteers helping civilians, but the threat of military escalation if forces in Syria don't stop the use of chemical weapons or cooperate with beneficent endeavors like the circulating of food to civilians.

In short: People had three choices. War, peace, or war if peace fails; defaulting to a fight, defaulting to running from the fight, or doing everything to avoid the fight but fighting if necessary. The choices were war, peace, or peace first; difficulty, ease, or trying the easy thing first but being ready to do the difficult thing if the easy one failed. People could "vote" for or against each plan. Now, they didn't have to "pass" any of them. If all 70 participants hated every plan, they could all vote no for each of them. They knew the rules.

The war plan failed. So did the peace plan. Both failed quite miserably. The peace first plan "passed" with 50 "yes votes."

KEY INSIGHT:

Don't Pursue the Hard Plan Unless the Easy One Won't Do.

VISUALIZING THE THREE TYPES OF PLANS

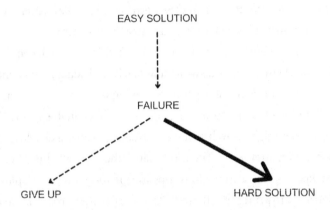

FIGURE 45: "Peace first" sees a problem, tries the easy solution, fails with the easy solution, tries the difficult solution, and fails or succeeds with it. "War" goes from problem to the difficult solution to failure or success. "Peace" goes from the problem to the easy solution to failure or success. The wisdom of the "peace first plan" (and remember, this is metaphorical) is this: "we'll try the easy fix first and if it doesn't work, we'll do whatever it takes."

Now, I'll leave this to you as an exercise. How do the findings of this little study reflect themselves in Clinton's language? And how can you extrapolate from this specific example a general rule of persuasion functioning in any situation? "We will act; with peaceful diplomacy whenever possible, with force when necessary."

PASSAGE #25:

But our greatest strength is the power of our ideas, which are still new in many lands. Across the world, we see them embraced, and we rejoice. Our hopes, our hearts, our hands, are with those on every continent who are building democracy and freedom. Their cause is America's cause.

SECRET #50:

How to activate social proof, turning on an irrevocably effective persuasive hot-button.

Social proof ranks amongst the most powerful individual persuasive inputs you can provide to your audience. People follow the crowd.

Social proof, a term coined by Robert Cialdini in his 1984 book, *Influence*, is also known as informational social influence. It describes a psychological and social phenomenon wherein people copy the actions of others in an attempt to undertake behavior in a given situation. And this is what Clinton activates when he says, "Across the world, we see them embraced, and we rejoice."

WHY DO WE FOLLOW THE CROWD?

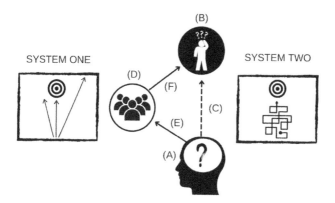

FIGURE 46: Prompted by a question (A), we seek to evaluate the target question of "what we should do" (B). However, this evaluation (C) is difficult. So, we substitute the heuristic question "what other people are doing" (D), evaluate this (E), and transfer the answer to the target question (F).

This is a fairly straightforward strategy: Present social proof, and instantly experience a tremendously persuasive pull toward your position, proposals, and ideas.

But the next secret shows you how to wrap social proof in a highly sophisticated structure: another proven, step-by-step triad producing predictable influence with ease.

PASSAGE #26:

The American people have summoned the change we celebrate today. You have raised your voices in an unmistakable chorus. You have cast your votes in historic numbers. And you have changed the face of Congress, the presidency and the political process itself. Yes, you, my fellow Americans have forced the spring. Now, we must do the work the season demands.

SECRET #51:

How to use the demand-opportunity-satisfaction triad to build an effortlessly effective message.

This is yet another simple three-step structure for delivering massive persuasive impact. And here's the key: It specifically meshes well with calls to action.

First, explain the demand people have and express the social proof behind this demand. Second, explain your new opportunity created to satisfy this demand. Third, tell them it takes action on their part to satisfy the demand by using the new opportunity.

THE PERSUASIVE VORTEX OF THE "DOS" TRIAD

FIGURE 47: Demand creates social proof for the opportunity. The opportunity establishes the need for action; the opportunity must be acted upon.

"*(Demand)* The American people have summoned the change we celebrate today. You have raised your voices in an unmistakable chorus. You have cast your votes in historic numbers. *(New opportunity)* And you have changed the face of Congress, the presidency and the political process itself. Yes, you, my fellow Americans have forced the spring. *(Satisfaction)* Now, we must do the work the season demands."

PASSAGE #27:

To that work I now turn, with all the authority of my office. I ask the Congress to join with me. But no president, no Congress, no government, can undertake this mission alone. My fellow Americans, you, too, must play your part in our renewal. I challenge a new generation of young Americans to a season of service; to act on your idealism by helping troubled children, keeping company with those in need, reconnecting our torn communities. There is so much to be done; enough indeed for millions of others who are still young in spirit to give of themselves in service, too.

SECRET #52:

How to avoid a mistake capable of rendering the rest of your persuasive efforts useless.

If you don't do this one thing, nothing else matters. It will all amount to a big pile of nothing. You must provide a call to action. A call to action is exactly what it sounds like: You are calling them to take a specific action, giving them a clear and direct call to either accept or reject.

WHY YOU MUST PROVIDE A CALL TO ACTION

FIGURE 48: You must accomplish the five steps in their order. If the process falls apart, it does so at its weakest link: the step you executed least effectively.

The mistake is forgetting to use one, or thinking it's too direct. Yes: You want to be strategic, subtle, and avoid aggressive and blunt persuasion. But at the same time, people have to know what you want from them. Don't beat them over the head with it, but make it clear. A confused mind always says no.

In this section, Clinton calls people to take specific actions. Action-oriented language is critical because it does something with the persuasive momentum built prior, channeling it in a real, practical direction. But at the same time, if you don't build the persuasive momentum, people won't take the action, even though you've called them to. You need both. Take this less as a secret and more as a warning.

PASSAGE #28:

In serving, we recognize a simple but powerful truth, we need each other. And we must care for one another. Today, we do more than celebrate America; we rededicate ourselves to the very idea of America.

SECRET #53:

How to achieve easy emotional resonance by taking the role of the inner-spokesperson.

This strategy is ubiquitous in the communication of legendary leaders. They all do it, and to great effect. When you use it, people allow you to dictate, to a degree, their mindset in approaching the subject you're speaking about.

How do you execute this strategy? How do you take the role of the inner-spokesperson? It has to do with these "we" statements. They achieve instant emotional resonance because Clinton describes shared experiences of an essentially emotional nature: "In serving, *we recognize* a simple but powerful truth, we need each other. We *rededicate ourselves* to the very idea of America."

It's not you should do this; it's we are already doing this. It's a much more compelling and effective way of changing an audience's mental state. Implicitly take on the role of the spokesperson for the group and make statements that basically follow this simple, straightforward, and easy format: "We [insert emotional experience dictating a mental state conducive to your persuasion]."

It's a mental shift. Recognizing something is a mental shift; rededicating yourself is a mental shift.

If he wanted people to feel angry at Ronald Reagan, for example, he could have said, "We reject the broken policies of Reaganomics." It works because reject is an emotionally implicative word suggesting avoidance, and because it is a mental shift.

PASSAGE #29:

An idea born in revolution and renewed through two centuries of challenge. An idea tempered by the knowledge that, but for fate we, the fortunate and the unfortunate, might have been each other. An idea ennobled by the faith that our nation can summon from its myriad diversity the deepest measure of unity. An idea infused with the conviction that America's long heroic journey must go forever upward.

SECRET #54:

How to appeal to the desire for certainty to instantly create a compelling attraction to your offer with an easy strategy.

Check out this first sentence: "An idea born in revolution and renewed through two centuries of challenge."

Now, compare these two much less sacred phrases: "This investing course teaches you strategies to build a crash-proof portfolio," and "This investing course teaches you proven, time-tested, reliable strategies to predictably build a crash-proof portfolio, guaranteed in any investing climate."

Which of those two is more compelling? The second. Why? Because it uses words to create a sense of certainty about the offering. And it invokes the same psychological need as Clinton's language, which sought to create a sense of certainty about the idea of America itself.

PASSAGE #30:

And so, my fellow Americans, at the edge of the 21st century, let us begin with energy and hope, with faith and discipline, and let us work until our work is done. The scripture says, 'And let us not be weary in well-doing, for in due season, we shall reap, if we faint not.'

SECRET #55:

How to use "soft" calls to action to persuade in nearly 100% of situations with a near-100% success-rate.

A "hard" call to action is calling for a specific, clear, tangible action. A "soft" call to action is calling for a mindset shift; an approach to life; a way of thinking. You can quite literally persuade in nearly 100% of situations with a near-100% success-rate if you apply a secondary call to action supporting your tangible one.

Now, your best-case is getting people to take the hard-call to action. It is even better if they follow the soft one too. But for those who don't follow the hard call to action, they can still follow the soft call to action. What was Clinton's soft call to action? "...let us begin with energy and hope, with faith and discipline..."

PASSAGE #31:

From this joyful mountaintop of celebration, we hear a call to service in the valley. We have heard the trumpets. We have changed the guard. And now, each in our way, and with God's help, we must answer the call. Thank you, and God bless you all.

SECRET #56:

How to paint your call to action as a moral imperative, creating a much more compelling persuasive "approach" pull.

This passage applies the spectrum of the sacred and profane to the call to action, turning it from an everyday request to a moral imperative, emanating from a higher plane of existence.

Anyone can use this with some creativity.

For example, an investing course marketer could change the call-to-action button (which web-visitors click if they want to purchase) from "Buy now!" to "Yes! I want to learn how to achieve freedom, peace of mind, and financial stability to provide for my family."

.............................Chapter Summary.................................

- You must begin with a hook that captivates attention in a way that sets the foundation for your message.
- Offer people a paradigm shift; rally them behind a totally new, groundbreaking, and exciting movement.
- Influence occurs at every scale of meaning: Even individual words standing alone contribute semantic sentiment.
- Characterize the moment in an advantageous way: as a moment of decision or opportunity, for example.
- People move to escape pain, attain pleasure, or replace pain with pleasure. These are the three fundamental motivations.
- Problems exist in three forms: externally, internally (as the pain the externals cause), and as problems of injustice.

GIVING THE GIFT OF MEANING

"What feats he did that day: then shall our names.
Familiar in his mouth as household words
Harry the king, Bedford and Exeter,
Warwick and Talbot, Salisbury and Gloucester,
Be in their flowing cups freshly remember'd.
This story shall the good man teach his son;
And Crispin Crispian shall ne'er go by,
From this day to the ending of the world,
But we in it shall be remember'd;
We few, we happy few, we band of brothers;"
- King Henry in Shakespeare's Henry V

a small number of lucky people

united in their devotion to each other

and to a mission worth remembering

MEANING

YOUR PERSUASIVE TOOLBOX (PART TWO)

1	Use Eisenhower's Rhetorical Secrets
1.1	Appeal to Psychological Self-Identity
1.2	Form a Psychological Coalition
1.3	Activate the Primacy Effect
1.4	Use the Principle of Persuasive Consistency
1.5	Present Contextual Pre-framing
1.6	Call Out Your Audience By Their Salient Identity
1.7	Apply the Sacred-Profane Spectrum
1.8	Use Aristotle's 2,000-Year-Old Persuasive Key
1.9	Instigate Broad-Based Emotional "Mood Shifts"
1.10	Present a Future-Based Cause
1.11	Remember to Introduce High Stakes
1.12	Reverse-Engineer the Sunk-Cost Fallacy
1.13	Apply the Values, Beliefs, Policies Triad
1.14	Recognize and Use Connotative Coded Imagery
1.15	Justify Your Persuasive Narrative by Confronting a Problem
1.16	Apply the Problem, Agitate, Solution Structure
1.17	Divulge the Brutal Truth
1.18	Wrap Up the Foundational Structure with Contrast
1.19	Apply Emotional-Sentiment-Agitation Aimed at the Solution

THE SCAFFOLD OF PERSUASION

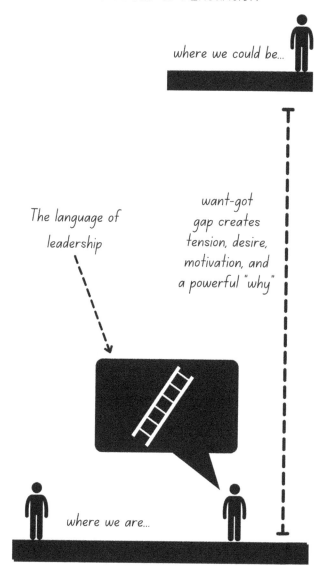

THE ARCHETYPAL PERSUASIVE MESSAGE

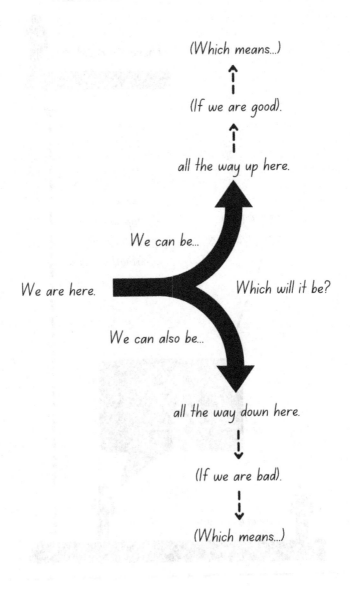

(Which means...)

↑

(If we are good).

↑

all the way up here.

We can be...

We are here.

We can also be...

Which will it be?

all the way down here.

↓

(If we are bad).

↓

(Which means...)

Claim These Free Resources that Will Help You Unleash the Power of Your Words and Speak with Confidence. Visit www.speakforsuccesshub.com/toolkit for Access.

18 Free PDF Resources

12 Iron Rules for Captivating Story, 21 Speeches that Changed the World, 341-Point Influence Checklist, 143 Persuasive Cognitive Biases, 17 Ways to Think On Your Feet, 18 Lies About Speaking Well, 137 Deadly Logical Fallacies, 12 Iron Rules For Captivating Slides, 371 Words that Persuade, 63 Truths of Speaking Well, 27 Laws of Empathy, 21 Secrets of Legendary Speeches, 19 Scripts that Persuade, 12 Iron Rules For Captivating Speech, 33 Laws of Charisma, 11 Influence Formulas, 219-Point Speech-Writing Checklist, 21 Eloquence Formulas

Claim These Free Resources that Will Help You Unleash the Power of Your Words and Speak with Confidence. Visit <u>www.speakforsuccesshub.com/toolkit</u> for Access.

30 Free Video Lessons

We'll send you one free video lesson every day for 30 days, written and recorded by Peter D. Andrei. Days 1-10 cover authenticity, the prerequisite to confidence and persuasive power. Days 11-20 cover building self-belief and defeating communication anxiety. Days 21-30 cover how to speak with impact and influence, ensuring your words change minds instead of falling flat. Authenticity, self-belief, and impact – this course helps you master three components of confidence, turning even the most high-stakes presentations from obstacles into opportunities.

Claim These Free Resources that Will Help You Unleash the Power of Your Words and Speak with Confidence. Visit www.speakforsuccesshub.com/toolkit for Access.

2 Free Workbooks

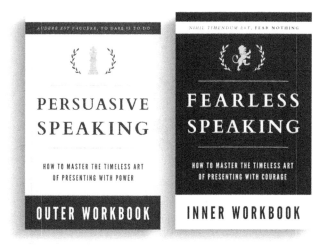

We'll send you two free workbooks, including long-lost excerpts by Dale Carnegie, the mega-bestselling author of *How to Win Friends and Influence People* (5,000,000 copies sold). *Fearless Speaking* guides you in the proven principles of mastering your inner game as a speaker. *Persuasive Speaking* guides you in the time-tested tactics of mastering your outer game by maximizing the power of your words. All of these resources complement the Speak for Success collection.

SPEAK FOR SUCCESS COLLECTION BOOK

XIII

THE LANGUAGE OF LEADERSHIP CHAPTER

IV

DURING STAGNATION:
Ronald Reagan's 1976 Convention Address

"THEY WILL KNOW WHETHER WE MET OUR CHALLENGE..."

IF YOU'RE PASSIONATE ABOUT POLITICS, you probably dislike Reagan and like Clinton, like Reagan and dislike Clinton, or dislike them both.

And yet, Ronald Reagan was known as "The Great Communicator." His words are more alive today than ever before, continuing to define the fundamental ethos of his party.

He was one of the most impactful political leaders and persuaders in American history. The masterful perfection with which he communicated is shocking. The political conversations we have today are still insurmountably influenced by him.

So, you might not like him. That's fine. Or, you might love him and dislike Clinton. That's fine too. But the question is this: Are you going to let that stop you from learning their techniques?

Hopefully the answer is no.

PASSAGE #1:

Mr. President, Mrs. Ford, Mr. Vice President, Mr. Vice President-to-be, the distinguished guests here, you ladies and gentlemen. I was going to say fellow Republicans here but those who are watching from a distance including all those millions of Democrats and independents who I know are looking for a cause around which to rally and which I believe we can give them. Mr. President, before you arrive tonight, these wonderful people, here, when we came in, gave Nancy and myself a welcome. That, plus this, plus your kindness and generosity in honoring us by bringing us down here will give us a memory that will live in our hearts forever.

SECRET #57:

How to use inclusivity-indicators to drastically and dramatically broaden your sphere of influence.

Inclusivity-indicators are short phrases that paint a straightforward picture: "You're all welcome here. This solution – this idea – it works for all of us."

While the other persuasive secrets discovered so far largely deal with raising the degree to which you influence the people in your persuasive funnel, this one deals with increasing the number of people who enter the funnel in the first place.

BROADENING THE FUNNEL VERSUS STRENGTHENING IT

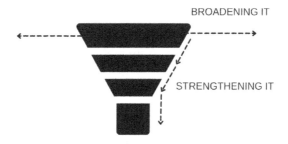

FIGURE 49: Broadening the persuasive funnel increases the number of people who enter it. Strengthening it increases the number of people who, upon entering it, flow deeper into it, as well as raising the speed of this.

How did Reagan use this strategy? "I was going to say fellow Republicans here but those who are watching from a distance including all those millions of Democrats and independents who I know are looking for a cause around which to rally and which I believe we can give them."

The message is simple: Join us. You're welcome here. We can give you what you're looking for, even if you always saw yourself as diametrically opposed to everything we stand for. We can talk this through. We aren't enemies.

This is the inclusivity approach. It seeks to reach out to the other side and bridge the gap between them in rhetoric, but not necessarily in real policy considerations.

There is also the antagonistic approach. It seeks to throw stones at the other side and solidify the strength of influence over those already in the camp, rather than trying to get more people in the camp.

But, more broadly, this hints at the strategy of eliminating people's pre-existing psychological objections, and doing so preemptively.

Whenever you try to get people to do anything, even to listen to you, they have their own unique objections in mind. Over time, patterns emerge, and you can begin to understand the core objections keeping most people from taking action or listening to you in the first place.

"Even if" constructions address the objections once you find them. These are short phrases following the portrayal of your central proposal designed to address the most compelling objections you predict. It's saying, "Here's my idea, and here's why it works even if you have no experience with this type of thing, even if you have no time to apply it, even if..." listing through all the major objections.

The inclusivity approach is essentially an implied "even if" construction; it essentially says, "Yes, this is for you, even if you're a Democrat (addressing the 'I'm a Democrat' objection)."

As such, it preemptively lifts an obstacle on the road from unconvinced to persuaded. And what's your job as a persuader? Clearing all the obstacles on that road, and gently helping your audience members follow it through to its end.

SECRET #58:

How to achieve likeability to make yourself more persuasive in any situation.

This speech was a more personal affair than an inaugural address. This made it perfect for striving to create likeability. If you recall, Robert Cialdini, in his groundbreaking book *Influence: The Psychology of Persuasion*, presents likeability as one of the six core elements of persuasion.

In short: People are more likely to be persuaded by you if they like you. And people like those with similar goals and similar life experiences; those they can identify with, who reflect elements of themselves (identification). They also like those who portray virtues in natural ways (idealization) and those who compliment and honor them (sentiment-reciprocation).

THE THREE COMPONENTS OF LIKEABILITY

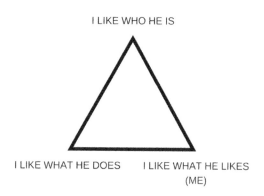

I LIKE WHO HE IS

I LIKE WHAT HE DOES   I LIKE WHAT HE LIKES
(ME)

FIGURE 50: While likeability is complex, this three-part rubric provides a robust starting framework.

Reagan portrayed virtues like gratitude and humility with language like this: "Mr. President, before you arrive tonight, these wonderful people, here, when we came in, gave Nancy and myself a welcome. That, plus this, plus your kindness and generosity in honoring us by bringing us down here will give us a memory that will live in our hearts forever."

He honors key guests when he says this: "Mr. President, Mrs. Ford, Mr. Vice President, Mr. Vice President-to-be, the distinguished guests here, you ladies and gentlemen."

You might think these short pleasantries matter little, but that's not true. If they establish likeability, they can create a positive halo effect lasting long into the future and getting your audience to view everything else you say through a dramatically more positive lens, yielding significantly better persuasive results.

KEY INSIGHT:

The Greatest Way to Receive Respect Is by Showing It. The Greatest Way to Receive Goodwill Is by Giving It. And the Greatest Way to Earn Attention Is ny Paying It: To Your Audience, To Your Message, And To the Present Moment.

PASSAGE #2:

Watching on television these last few nights I've seen also the warmth with which you greeted Nancy and you also filled my heart with joy when you did that. May I say some words. There are cynics who say that a party platform is something that no one bothers to read and is doesn't very often amount to much. Whether it is different this time than it has ever been before, I believe the Republican party has a platform that is a banner of bold, unmistakable colors with no pale pastel shades. We have just heard a call to arms, based on that platform.

SECRET #59:

How to use the two-step belief-contrast structure to immediately make people see things your way.

We talked about contrast before. This simple two-step structure uses contrast to great effect. It also uses aspirational persuasion; persuading through the casting of attractive aspirations they want to strive toward.

It's a simple structure. What does it do? It defeats objections, guarantees people don't fall into the wrong pattern of thoughts (that is, patterns unlikely to lead to the action you want), and leads people to the point of view you prefer.

It goes like this: First, enumerate the inferior belief about the subject, usually containing some objection, and describe the associated mental state. Second, transition to your clearly superior belief about the subject, a perfect contrast of the inferior belief, and a belief obviously much more attractive.

The goal? Move people from the first inferior belief to the second superior belief.

Here's how Reagan did it: *"(Enumerating the first and inferior belief)* There are cynics who say that a party platform is something that no one bothers to read and is doesn't very often amount to much. *(Transitioning to and enumerating the superior contrasting belief)* Whether it is different this time than is has ever been before, I believe the Republican party has a platform that is a banner of bold, unmistakable colors with no pale pastel shades."

He didn't present the first, objection-riddled belief and say, "Which is obviously wrong! Don't think this!" He didn't present his superior belief and say, "Now this... *this* is the way to go!" He didn't present both and then say, "So, what I want you to think is..."

Instead, he allowed the contrast between the beliefs and the self-evident superiority of the second one to do his work for him. Just by presenting them together in this way, he made the choice easy, clear, and obvious. Cynicism (belief one), or hope (belief two)? Most people see hope as the obvious choice.

And why do this at all? Because it is essential to persuasion. Reagan deemed it essential to defeat the first mental state (cynicism about party platforms – an objection to the rest of his message) and move people to adopt the second mental state (hope about party platforms – a prerequisite to being persuaded by the rest of his message).

Here's a simple language pattern to apply this structure: "There are some people who believe (insert objection). On the other hand, we believe (insert superior pattern of beliefs)."

Let's bring back the example of the investing course. Let's say you're the marketing manager for this product. How would you apply this structure? First, identify a common objection. For example, "Investing is too volatile." Second, complete the first half of the structure built around what you just identified: "Some anxious people out there say they will never invest and strive for financial independence because the markets are just too volatile." Third, identify the contrasting superior belief to this limiting, objection-based belief. For example, "Investing correctly isn't volatile." Fourth, complete the second half of the structure built around what you just identified: "The more aware individuals know that with the correct knowledge and the proper training from trading experts, risk and volatility can be completely mitigated and financial independence can be theirs."

What do we arrive at? "Some anxious people out there say they will never invest and strive for financial independence because the markets are just too volatile. The more aware individuals know that with the correct knowledge and the proper training from trading experts, risk and volatility can be completely mitigated and financial independence can be theirs."

See how this naturally moves people from the first, objection-based and inferior belief, to the second empowering belief? The key is the obvious superiority of the second belief. Hope is obviously superior to cynicism, and the understanding that correct knowledge can hedge against volatility is obviously superior to mistakenly fearing volatility and not investing as a result.

To subtly drive home the obviousness of the second belief's superiority, you can use connotative language at the sentence level. The first belief is held by "anxious people" who "say" they will "never invest and strive for financial independence," while the second belief is held by "the more aware individuals" who "know" that "financial independence can be theirs."

And you can stack this structure upon itself, turning it into a basic building block for a persuasive tower, hitting objection after objection – hitting limiting-belief after limiting-belief – replacing them with the superior beliefs which will empower people to accept your call to action in a sequence.

SECRET #60:

How to use the hidden, little-known visualization pathway to grab attention and easily paint persuasive pictures.

If you read the passage closely, one phrase probably grabbed your attention: "Whether it is different this time than it has ever been before, I believe the Republican party has a platform that is a *banner of bold, unmistakable colors with no pale pastel shades.*"

Why is it so captivating? Because our minds cannot help but see these images when we read the words symbolizing them.

Yellow.

You probably just, in your mind's eye, imagined the color yellow. This image-infusion into your mental movie-projector captivated your attention.

The world's most legendary works of literature are ripe with visually stimulating descriptions and visual metaphors. These techniques flood our minds with clear visualizations, drawing us into the story.

The advantages are vast: Visual language is memorable, captivating, persuasive, intuitive, and effective no matter how you measure it.

And this is a step beyond simple image-infusions, because it is a visual metaphor; it's an analogy, so it proves a substantive point.

Guess what people are going to remember for days, months, and even years after hearing this speech? This phrase: "The Republican party has a platform that is a banner of bold, unmistakable colors with no pale pastel shades." Now you know why. And it's a good phrase for people to remember and replay in their heads (if you're Reagan), isn't it?

SECRET #61:

How to use the VAKOG senses to instantly draw people into your communication and command undivided attention.

While using the visual pathway is a particularly compelling way to get attention and share a message memorably, the other senses work well too.

The senses are broken down in the VAKOG framework: Visual, auditory, kinesthetic, olfactory, gustatory; or, more simply, sight, sound, the feeling of your body, smell, and taste.

Use them. Reagan used the auditory sense when he said, "We have just *heard* a call to arms, based on that platform." Now, this could have been improved by making the sense-invocation more specific: "We have just *heard a trumpet call* to arms, based on that platform." Most people know the sound of a trumpet, and the more specific the sense-invocation, the more vivid the listening experience, and thus the more attention-grabbing and memorable it is.

There are two simple ways to use these. First, share stories in which the protagonist (someone the audience can identify with, feel sympathy for, or otherwise root for) sees, feels, smells, hears, and tastes particular things. Embed a key insight in the story, so it serves a persuasive purpose. And remember, be creative: They don't have to be eating food in the story for you to invoke the taste sense. They can taste bitter adrenalin. They can taste sour defeat. Be metaphorical and figurative.

Second, include attached VAKOG adjectives or micro-VAKOG metaphors to nouns and verbs. An attached VAKOG adjective is an adjective directly preceding the noun or verb it modifies, and an adjective invoking one of the VAKOG senses. "This young candidate offers a vision for a better future" becomes "This *bright* young candidate offers a *shining* vision for the future." A micro-VAKOG metaphor is a short metaphor based on one of the five senses. "This young candidate offers a vision for a future" becomes "This young candidate offers a vision for *the next blank page in our story (a concrete, physical, specific item that can be visualized)."*

In *The Political Brain,* Drew Westen boils down all of political persuasion into first, competing narratives, and second, neural networks of association between different concepts (for example, politicians should form neural networks of associations between the opposing party and bad things and their party and good things).

In *Thinking Fast and Slow,* Daniel Kahneman discusses the availability bias: We overweigh information we remember quickly, fluently, confidently and completely; in other words, we overweigh information that is readily available. It influences us to an outsized degree.

Well, using these previous two secrets forms persuasive neural networks of association. For example, Reagan creates a neural association between the Republican party and strong, direct principles. However, because he embeds this sentiment in a visual metaphor, it becomes a particularly strong and particularly persuasive neural network. At the same time, due to their vivid, experiential nature, statements of this kind are extremely memorable. Thus, they activate the availability bias in your favor as well.

PASSAGE #3:

And a call to us to really be successful in communicating and reveal to the American people the difference between this platform and the platform of the opposing party which is nothing but a revamp and a reissue and a rerunning of a late, late show of the thing that we have been hearing from them for the last 40 years.

SECRET #62:

How to use the path-contrast strategy to avoid persuasion that falls flat and fails to influence.

It doesn't matter how incredible your proposal is. That's not what matters. Persuasion is the act of getting people to act, and all action is based on deciding between alternative actions.

Build up your proposal. But remember that the key is how it stacks up to available alternatives. It can be the best thing since sliced bread, but if the alternative it's going up against happens to be sliced bread, it doesn't matter, does it? You've lost.

Speakers forget to positively contrast their idea – their proposed action – with the other available alternatives, thus forgetting to answer the most important question: "Is it the best way forward?"

That is what people are asking themselves. Indeed, that's what they should be asking themselves. It doesn't matter if you can convince them your proposed action is good; it matters if you can convince them it is the best option available.

REVEALING ONE OF THE MOST POWERFUL NARRATIVES

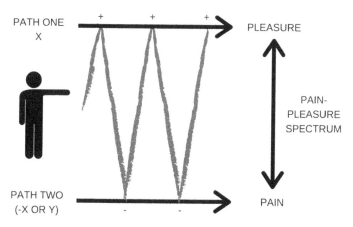

FIGURE 51: The aforementioned path contrast strategy works because of the contrast effect. The pleasure caused

by "path one" appears more positive and vivid when placed
next to the pain caused by "path two," and vice-versa.

Remember this: Don't answer "Why is it good?" Answer "Why is
it the best?" And how does Reagan do this? It's self-evident in this
passage, isn't it? The entire passage is focused on conveying the
following idea: "Not only are we good; *we're better than all the other
options you have.*"

Persuasion – logical persuasion, at least – revolves around
convincing people not that "doing X is good," but that "doing X is
the best possible thing you can do at this point in time." Don't get the
two mixed up. Keep your true objective crystal-clear. Remember this:
Logical persuasion is based on the word "best." Tell people why
doing what you want them to do is the best thing they can do.

KEY INSIGHT:

"It's Good" Doesn't Matter If Every Option Is. What Matters Is How an Option Stacks Up Against Available Alternatives

The World of Influence Revolves Around the Word "Best."

PASSAGE #4:

If I could just take a moment, I had an assignment the other day. Someone asked me to write a letter for a time capsule that is going to be opened in Los Angeles a hundred years from now, on our Tricentennial.

SECRET #63:

How to use the trojan-horse storytelling technique to immediately hook any audience.

Don't simply state your key persuasive idea; instead, embed the key persuasive idea in a captivating, compelling story (either about yourself or someone else), and share the story itself.

Why is it called the Trojan-Horse storytelling technique? Because the Greeks (you) ended the Trojan War (persuasion resistance) by offering a hollow wooden horse (the story) as a peace offering to Troy (your audience), getting it behind their walls (their conscious filter), with Greek soldiers (your persuasive message) hidden in the horse's frame.

In short: Your audience is so wrapped up in the story, they can't even see past it, and your persuasive message covertly converts them. Done right, this strategy will get people to realize your message themselves (as you're telling the story), which is much more effective than telling them the message flatly.

KEY INSIGHT:

Facts Tell. Stories Show. Facts Convey. Stories Convince.

WHAT MAKES A STORY WORTH TELLING?

ATTACKING DIRECTLY

THE TROJAN HORSE
TECHNIQUE

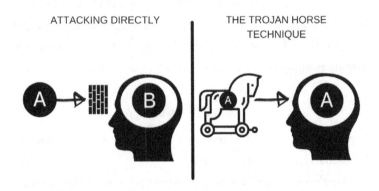

FIGURE 52: Instead of approaching your persuasive prospects by flatly stating the core persuasive epiphany you would like them to adopt, embed this persuasive epiphany in a story that will give them the ingredients to experience the belief-shift themselves.

First, identify what core epiphany, idea, or realization you want people to adopt. Second, remember when you first had this realization. Third, tell them this story. They'll have the same realization as you do in the story.

Pacing and leading is a related principle. Want to change someone from believing X to believing Y? Don't just go in there and say "Y." It won't work. First, you have to pace them; you have to match them where they are (X) before you can lead them and move to them to where you are (Y). How? By telling a story with this basic structure: "I used to think the same exact thing: X. Here's why I used to think X. But then, something happened. Here's the emotional, compelling, and captivating personal story that turned me from thinking X to thinking Y."

Humans love stories. Stories are inherently intuitive ways to package information. Stories captivate us. We passed down components of cultural evolution for thousands of years through stories, myths, and legends. We artificially organize the world into narratives to tame its overwhelming complexity.

So, not only is it an incredibly compelling persuasive technique for influencing people to have the realization you want them to have, it is also an incredibly compelling persuasive technique for persuading people to listen to you in the first place.

Typically, when you hear someone start to tell a story, don't your ears perk up? Don't you lean in and listen? For example, when Reagan says, "If I could just take a moment, I had an assignment the other day. Someone asked me to write a letter for a time capsule that is going to be opened in Los Angeles a hundred years from now, on our Tricentennial," don't you feel inclined to listen? Don't you feel like it's a promise of entertainment instead of a sign of dry, boring, direct attempts at influencing you? Don't you feel the invitation into a story – assuming it's from a good storyteller (and Reagan was) – is like a little break from the struggles of life, and a short moment to forget yourself and experience the world through someone else's eyes (which, in this particular moment, just so happen to be seeing whatever first convinced them to think how they want you to think now)? Of course, this is just the start of the story. Watch it develop over the following passages.

PASSAGE #5:

It sounded like an easy assignment. They suggested I write about the problems and issues of the day. And I set out to do so, riding down the coast in an automobile, looking at the blue Pacific out on one side and the Santa Ynez Mountains on the other, and I couldn't help but wonder if it was going to be that beautiful a hundred years from now as it was on that summer day.

SECRET #64:

How to use open loops to play on innate human curiosity and command complete attention.

There are two ways to use curiosity in your persuasive efforts. Remember: All persuasion demands first persuading them to listen, and then persuading them to act on what they heard. First, you can use curiosity to persuade them to listen. Second, you can use curiosity to persuade them to act, by placing the knowledge you teased and aroused curiosity about on the other side of the action. "Want to know X? Do Y," essentially. (Not in those words, of course, but that is the basic sentiment).

Reagan used curiosity, in this case, to persuade people to keep listening to his story. How? With an open loop; an unanswered question; a half-finished riddle. And it commands attention like nothing else.

HOW TO GRAB INSTANT ATTENTION

SET OF POSSIBLE KNOWLEDGE

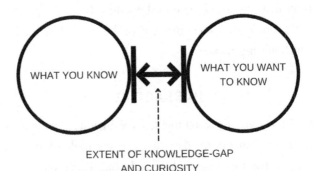

EXTENT OF KNOWLEDGE-GAP
AND CURIOSITY

FIGURE 53: Presenting a gap between knowledge and desired knowledge instigates curiosity and grabs attention.

"I couldn't help but wonder if it was going to be that beautiful a hundred years from now as it was on that summer day." Now we can't either, Reagan. So, we'll listen even more closely for any clues.

PASSAGE #6:

And then as I tried to write – let your own minds turn to that task. You're going to write for people a hundred years from now who know all about us, we know nothing about them. We don't know what kind of world they'll be living in. And suddenly I thought to myself, If I write of the problems, they'll be the domestic problems of which the President spoke here tonight; the challenges confronting us, the erosion of freedom taken place under Democratic rule in this country, the invasion of private rights, the controls and restrictions on the vitality of the great free economy that we enjoy. These are the challenges that we must meet and then again there is that challenge of which he spoke that we live in a world in which the great powers have aimed and poised at each other horrible missiles of destruction, nuclear weapons that can in a matter of minutes arrive at each other's country and destroy virtually the civilized world we live in.

SECRET #65:

How to use the hidden, little-known strategy of counterfactual simulation for instant influence.

In *The Personal MBA*, Josh Kauffman says the following about counterfactual simulation: "Counterfactual simulation is applied imagination: Consciously asking a "what if" question, and letting your mind imagine the rest. Based on the stored patterns, associations and interpretations, your brain will produce what it believes is the most likely scenario. Counterfactuals are very useful because of their flexibility: You can simulate anything you want. When you use counterfactual simulation, you assume the event or state you're simulating is already true. The mind then fills the gaps between A (where you are) and B (where you want to be)."

Counterfactual simulation is incredibly captivating. It draws people in. Daydreams are often counterfactual simulations. When people are lost in thought, oblivious to their surroundings, they are often intently focused on a counterfactual simulation.

Invite your audience into a counterfactual simulation. Invite your audience to imagine something. Our brains are extremely adept at creating vivid and realistic simulations. It's a powerful way to make a point and grab attention in the process.

Here's how Reagan did it: "And then as I tried to write – let your own minds turn to that task. You're going to write for people a hundred years from now who know all about us, we know nothing about them. We don't know what kind of world they'll be living in."

When he said this, he made the communication mentally interactive; he made it tactile and active as opposed to passive; he made it captivating, helping the audience simulate a scene inspiring them to adopt the preconditions for accepting his persuasive appeals.

SECRET #66:

How to use rhetorical climax to put people in an emotional state of desperately needing what you offer.

Rhetorical climax is a tool for agitation. Make statements of the same essential sentiment (for example, in Reagan's case, all examples of "the domestic problems of which the President spoke here tonight; the challenges confronting us"), and arrange them in order of increasing intensity, going from least intense to most intense; from lowest-stakes to highest-stakes.

Observe how Reagan raises the intensity with each of the examples: "And suddenly I thought to myself, If I write of the problems, they'll be the domestic problems of which the President spoke here tonight; the challenges confronting us, *the erosion of freedom taken place under Democratic rule in this country, the invasion of private rights, the controls and restrictions on the vitality of the great free economy that we enjoy.* These are the challenges that we must meet and then again there is that challenge of which he spoke that *we live in a world in which the great powers have aimed and poised at each other horrible missiles of destruction, nuclear weapons that can in a matter of minutes arrive at each other's country and destroy virtually the civilized world we live in.*"

It's leading with the bad – the domestic problems like decreased freedom, increased economic restriction, and decreased individual rights – and then jumping to the terrible: the destruction of the world "in a matter of minutes." Use this for emotional agitation as part of the PAS structure (or any structure for that matter – agitation is a versatile strategy).

PASSAGE #7:

And suddenly it dawned on me; those who would read this letter a hundred years from now will know whether those missiles were fired. They will know whether we met our challenge.

SECRET #67:

How to present a moment of epiphany to cap off your story and get people to perfectly mirror your way of thinking.

In a previous secret, we discussed the Trojan-Horse storytelling model. We also discussed a particular form of this model: telling a story about your own life and the events that led you to the same realization – the same core persuasive epiphany – you want to inspire your audience to have.

Now, we see exactly how Reagan does just that: "And suddenly it dawned on me... (the realization)." That's all you have to say. If you built up the story correctly and anticipation for some sort of big breakthrough is high, all you have to say is something like, "And in that moment, I realized what eluded me for so long..."

This strategy hinges on your ability to recreate, both in your mind and in your audience's minds, the exact feeling you had when the realization came to you. Present all the milestones along the way; the feeling you're on the cusp of something; the little clues and teases; and then, after all that buildup, the big breakthrough itself.

SECRET #68:

How to apply the "future-significance today" method to make people feel morally obligated to act as you propose.

This passage also employs another compelling strategy: the "future-significance today" technique. Tell people today what their present actions will mean to people in the future. Show them how their current struggles look through "the eye of history."

This strategy motivates them to hold fast and continually strive forward with the understanding it'll mean something to people down the road. It's a strategy designed to reinforce their sense of purpose when you perceive it might be waning, giving them the willpower boost to keep at it until they succeed.

How does Reagan execute it? "And suddenly it dawned on me; those who would read this letter a hundred years from now will know whether those missiles were fired. They will know whether we met our challenge."

He tells them what's at stake for the people of tomorrow if they don't accomplish their mission today. And this can be an extremely persuasive way to get people to stick to their mission; telling them the suffering they, by virtue of their labor, will save for the next generation, and how the next generation will see them and their endeavor as a result.

VISUALIZING "THE EYE OF HISTORY" STRATEGY

NOW   +100 YEARS

FIGURE 54: Tell them how people a century later will perceive their struggle in the present moment. Put their present endeavor in the context of history. Tell them how the eye of history will see it.

PASSAGE #8:

Whether they will have the freedom that we have known up until now will depend on what we do here. Will they look back with appreciation and say, Thank God for those people in 1976 who headed off that loss of freedom? Who kept us now a hundred years later free? Who kept our world from nuclear destruction?"

SECRET #69:

How to use the "choose your future" mode of aspirational persuasion for easy influence.

In *Win Bigly*, Scott Adams names two critically powerful forms of persuasion: contrast persuasion (using contrasts typically between the proposed item and alternatives to suggest a particular action) and aspirational persuasion (connecting the audience's aspirations to the action you want them to take).

The "choose your future" mode is largely aspirational. Ask them if their future selves will look back and thank them for doing what you want them to do, or kick themselves out of regret for not doing it. "Will they look back with appreciation and say, 'Thank God for those people in 1976 who headed off that loss of freedom? Who kept us now a hundred years later free? Who kept our world from nuclear destruction?'" In this example, Reagan also combined this strategy with the eye of history approach.

Let's bring back the digital investing course. "20 years from now, will you be sitting on a portfolio worth hundreds of thousands of dollars, thanking yourself for taking this small chance today?"

Now you can easily layer contrast persuasion under it: "Or, will you regret missing the opportunity to reach for financial independence when you had the chance?"

PASSAGE #9:

And if we fail, they probably won't get to read the letter at all because it spoke of individual freedom and they won't be allowed to talk of that or read of it.

SECRET #70:

How to ethically use fear-based persuasion to create an irresistibly powerful psychological pull in your favor.

Fear is one of our most powerful motivating factors. We will do anything to escape our fears. And if you can connect your proposal to guaranteeing a fear doesn't manifest (or an alternative to guaranteeing one does), your persuasive pull will be tremendous.

In my view, it's not unethical if the connections to fear are real, and if the proposal is truly beneficial for the people adopting it. It's not unethical to use the fear caused by a fearsome problem to motivate people to solve the problem.

Observe how Reagan did it, and the gravity of the fears he invoked: "And if we fail, they probably won't get to read the letter at all because it spoke of individual freedom and *they won't be allowed to talk of that or read of it.*"

PASSAGE #10:

This is our challenge and this is why we're here in this hall tonight. Better than we've ever done before, we've got to quit talking to each other and about each other and go out and communicate to the world that we may be fewer in numbers than we've ever been but we carry the message they're waiting for. We must go forth from here united, determined and what a great general said a few years ago is true: There is no substitute for victory, Mr. President.

SECRET #71:

How to throw down a challenge to inspire people to act with enthusiasm and vigor.

In Dale Carnegie's mega-bestseller *How to Win Friends and Influence People*, he says that you can inspire people to act by "throwing down a challenge."

What does he mean by that? "The thing that most motivates people is the game. Everyone desires to excel and prove their worth. If we want someone to do something, we must give them a challenge and they will often rise to meet it."

As we can see in nearly every single example of a piece of legendary communication by a legendary leader, they use the language of challenges constantly to frame their proposals in an inherently motivating way: "This is our *challenge* and this is why we're here in this hall tonight..."

SECRET #72:

How to use the "all or nothing" approach to inspire fortitude in difficult times.

The art of persuasion hinges on understanding the psychology of the minds you're trying to move: the biases, blind-spots, and most importantly, likely objections (and the supporting arguments for these objections) to your idea.

And what is one of the most subtle and most common objections? It is more like a common belief-pattern from which hundreds of different objections can flow: the graduated-results assumption.

What is it? It's the belief that they can get some of the results they want on a spectrum; that they can land somewhere on a spectrum between "Yes! I did it!" and "I failed." This justifies inaction. Why? "Well, I could take this action and get the real results I want, but it might be hard, and there might be some risk associated with trusting this person. On the other hand, I could continue trying to get the results myself in a piece-meal fashion, and maybe get somewhere, even if it's not all the way to the summit."

So, what's the all or nothing approach? And how does it neutralize this belief-pattern?

It tosses aside the spectrum model. No: It's either a loss or a win. No in between. This makes the need for follow-through on your proposal much more evident. Why? There's no settling for something somewhere near victory; there's only defeat or victory, and they probably need to listen to you to get to victory.

How does Reagan use this strategy? "There is no substitute for victory, Mr. President."

Victory or defeat: No in between.

HOW TO RAISE THE STAKES OF THE GAME

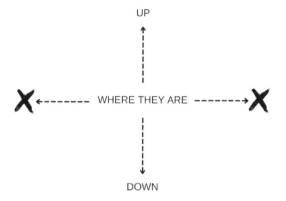

FIGURE 55: Win through to absolute, uncompromising victory. It's the only option.

...................................Chapter Summary...................................

- Inclusive language does not build barriers, including as many people as possible in the persuasive narrative.
- Humans perceive through contrasts. Various structures appeal to this, drawing contrasts to create emphasis.
- A rhetorical climax is a moment of peak intensity that drives home the essential persuasive message.
- Fear is a powerful motivator. Do not create fear; rather, channel preexisting fear as a motivator for positive action.
- Tell a story that embeds in itself the ingredients for your audience to arrive at your conclusion on their own.
- Present a moment of epiphany, detailing how you had a realization. Your audience will mirror the epiphany.

Claim These Free Resources that Will Help You Unleash the Power of Your Words and Speak with Confidence. Visit www.speakforsuccesshub.com/toolkit for Access.

18 Free PDF Resources

12 Iron Rules for Captivating Story, 21 Speeches that Changed the World, 341-Point Influence Checklist, 143 Persuasive Cognitive Biases, 17 Ways to Think On Your Feet, 18 Lies About Speaking Well, 137 Deadly Logical Fallacies, 12 Iron Rules For Captivating Slides, 371 Words that Persuade, 63 Truths of Speaking Well, 27 Laws of Empathy, 21 Secrets of Legendary Speeches, 19 Scripts that Persuade, 12 Iron Rules For Captivating Speech, 33 Laws of Charisma, 11 Influence Formulas, 219-Point Speech-Writing Checklist, 21 Eloquence Formulas

Claim These Free Resources that Will Help You Unleash the Power of Your Words and Speak with Confidence. Visit www.speakforsuccesshub.com/toolkit for Access.

30 Free Video Lessons

We'll send you one free video lesson every day for 30 days, written and recorded by Peter D. Andrei. Days 1-10 cover authenticity, the prerequisite to confidence and persuasive power. Days 11-20 cover building self-belief and defeating communication anxiety. Days 21-30 cover how to speak with impact and influence, ensuring your words change minds instead of falling flat. Authenticity, self-belief, and impact – this course helps you master three components of confidence, turning even the most high-stakes presentations from obstacles into opportunities.

YOUR PERSUASIVE TOOLBOX (PART THREE)

1	Use Eisenhower's Rhetorical Secrets
1.1	Appeal to Psychological Self-Identity
1.2	Form a Psychological Coalition
1.3	Activate the Primacy Effect
1.4	Use the Principle of Persuasive Consistency
1.5	Present Contextual Pre-framing
1.6	Call Out Your Audience By Their Salient Identity
1.7	Apply the Sacred-Profane Spectrum
1.8	Use Aristotle's 2,000-Year-Old Persuasive Key
1.9	Instigate Broad-Based Emotional "Mood Shifts"
1.10	Present a Future-Based Cause
1.11	Remember to Introduce High Stakes
1.12	Reverse-Engineer the Sunk-Cost Fallacy
1.13	Apply the Values, Beliefs, Policies Triad
1.14	Recognize and Use Connotative Coded Imagery
1.15	Justify Your Persuasive Narrative by Confronting a Problem
1.16	Apply the Problem, Agitate, Solution Structure
1.17	Divulge the Brutal Truth
1.18	Wrap Up the Foundational Structure with Contrast
1.19	Apply Emotional-Sentiment-Agitation Aimed at the Solution

2.14	Appeal to Human Loss-Aversion
2.15	Promise Means
2.16	Answer the "WIIFM?" Question
2.17	Dive Deep to the Core Human Desires at Play
2.18	Use the Frame-Escalation-Presentation Strategy
2.19	Reveal a Hidden Conspiracy
2.20	Speak to Broken-Justice Problems
2.21	Activate the Illusory Truth Effect
2.22	Apply a Tone of Self-Evidence
2.23	Use an "Or Else" Construction
2.24	Apply the Ease-Difficulty Duality
2.25	Activate Social Proof
2.26	Use the Demand, New Opportunity, Satisfaction Triad
2.27	Remember to Present a Call to Action
2.28	Take the Role of the Inner-Spokesperson
2.29	Create a Sense of Certainty
2.30	Paint Your Call to Action as a Moral Imperative
3	**Use Reagan's Rhetorical Secrets**
3.1	Use Inclusivity-Indicators
3.2	Achieve Likeability

3.3	Apply the Belief-Contrast Structure
3.4	Use the Visualization Pathway
3.5	Speak to the VAKOG Senses
3.6	Apply the Path-Contrast Structure
3.7	Use the Trojan-Horse Storytelling Technique
3.8	Create an Open Loop
3.9	Instigate a Counterfactual Simulation
3.10	Set Up a Rhetorical Climax
3.11	Present a Moment of Epiphany
3.12	Apply the Future-Significance Today Method
3.13	Use the "Choose Your Future" Mode of Persuasion
3.14	Apply Fear-Based Persuasion
3.15	Throw Down a Challenge
3.16	Use the All or Nothing Strategy

Email Peter D. Andrei, the author of the Speak for Success collection and the President of Speak Truth Well LLC directly.

pandreibusiness@gmail.com

SOMETHING WAS MISSING. THIS IS IT.

D ECEMBER OF 2021, I COMPLETED the new editions of the 15 books in the Speak for Success collection, after months of work, and many 16-hour-long writing marathons. The collection is over 1,000,000 words long and includes over 1,700 handcrafted diagrams. It is *the* complete communication encyclopedia. But instead of feeling relieved and excited, I felt uneasy and anxious. Why? Well, I know now. After writing over 1,000,000 words on communication across 15 books, it slowly dawned on me that I had missed the most important set of ideas about good communication. What does it *really* mean to be a good speaker? This is my answer.

THERE ARE THREE DIMENSIONS OF SUCCESS

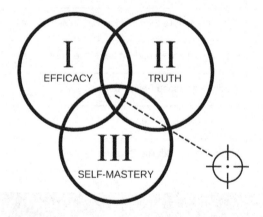

FIGURE I: A good speaker is not only rhetorically effective. They speak the truth, and they are students of self-mastery who experience peace, calm, and deep equanimity as they speak. These three domains are mutually reinforcing.

I realized I left out much about truth and self-mastery, focusing instead on the first domain. On page 33, the practical guide is devoted to domain I. On page 42, the ethical guide is devoted to domain II. We will shortly turn to domain III with an internal guide.

WHAT A GOOD SPEAKER LOOKS LIKE

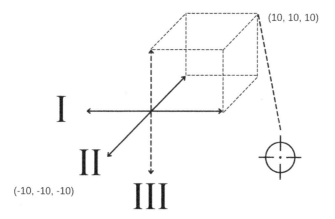

FIGURE II: We can conceptualize the three domains of success as an (X, Y, Z) coordinate plane, with each axis extending between -10 and 10. Your job is to become a (10, 10, 10). A (-10, 10, 10) speaks the truth and has attained self-mastery, but is deeply ineffective. A (10, -10, 10), speaks brilliantly and is at peace, but is somehow severely misleading others. A (10, 10, -10), speaks the truth well, but lives in an extremely negative inner state.

THE THREE AXES VIEWED DIFFERENTLY

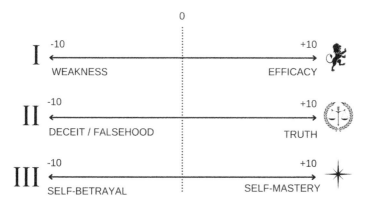

FIGURE III: We can also untangle the dimensions of improvement from representation as a coordinate plane, and instead lay them out flat, as spectrums of progress. A

(+10, -10, -10) is a true monster, eloquent but evil. A (10, 10, 10) is a Martin Luther King. A more realistic example is (4, -3, 0): This person is moderately persuasive, bends truth a little too much for comfort (but not horribly), and is mildly anxious about speaking but far from falling apart. Every speaker exists at some point along these axes.

THE EXTERNAL MASTERY PROCESS IS INTERNAL TOO

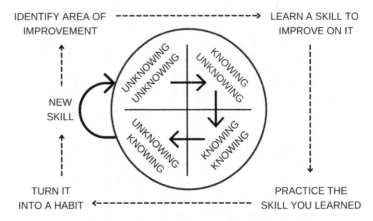

IDENTIFY AREA OF IMPROVEMENT -------------------> LEARN A SKILL TO IMPROVE ON IT

NEW SKILL

TURN IT INTO A HABIT <------------------------ PRACTICE THE SKILL YOU LEARNED

FIGURE IV: The same process presented earlier as a way to achieve rhetorical mastery will also help you achieve self-mastery. Just replace the word "skill" with "thought" or "thought-pattern," and the same cyclical method works.

THE THREE AXES, IN DIFFERENT WORDS

Domain One	Domain Two	Domain Three
Efficacy	Truth	Self-Mastery
Rhetoric	Research	Inner-Peace
Master of Words	Seeker of Truth	Captain of Your Soul
Aristotle's "Pathos"	Aristotle's "Logos"	Aristotle's "Ethos"
Impact	Insight	Integrity
Presence of Power	Proper Perspective	Power of Presence
Inter-Subjective	Objective	Subjective
Competency	Credibility	Character
External-Internal	External	Internal
Verbal Mastery	Subject Mastery	Mental Mastery
Behavioral	Cognitive	Emotional

THE POWER OF LANGUAGE

Language has generative power. This is why many creation stories include language as a primordial agent playing a crucial role in crafting reality. "In the beginning was the Word, and the Word was with God (John 1:1)."

Every problem we face has a story written about its future, whether explicit or implicit, conscious or subconscious. Generative language can rewrite a story that leads downward, turning it into one that aims us toward heaven, and then it can inspire us to realize this story. It can remove the cloud of ignorance from noble possibilities.

And this is good. You can orient your own future upward. That's certainly good for you. You can orient the future upward for yourself and for your family. That's better. And for your friends. That's better. And for your organization, your community, your city, and your country. That's better still. And for your enemies, and for people yet unborn; for all people, at all times, from now until the end of time.

And it doesn't get better than that.

Sound daunting? It is. It is the burden of human life. It is also the mechanism of moral progress. But start wherever you can, wherever you are. Start by acing your upcoming presentation.

But above all, remember this: all progress begins with truth.

Convey truth beautifully. And know thyself, so you can guard against your own proclivity for malevolence, and so you can strive toward self-mastery. Without self-mastery, it's hard, if not nearly impossible, to do the first part; to convey truth beautifully.

Truth, so you do good, not bad; impact, so people believe you; and self-mastery, as an essential precondition for truth and impact. Imagine what the world would be like if everyone were a triple-ten on our three axes. Imagine what good, what beauty, what bliss would define our existence. Imagine what good, what beauty, what bliss could define our existence, here and now.

It's up to you.

THE INNER GAME OF SPEAKING

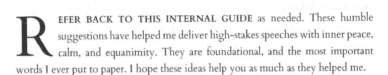

REFER BACK TO THIS INTERNAL GUIDE as needed. These humble suggestions have helped me deliver high-stakes speeches with inner peace, calm, and equanimity. They are foundational, and the most important words I ever put to paper. I hope these ideas help you as much as they helped me.

MASTER BOTH GAMES. Seek to master the outer game, but also the inner game. The self-mastery game comes before the word-mastery game, and even the world-mastery game. In fact, if you treat *any* game as a way to further your self-mastery, setting this as your "game above all games," you can never lose.

ADOPT THREE FOUNDATIONS. Humility: "The other people here probably know something I don't. They could probably teach me something. I could be overlooking something. I could be wrong. They have something to contribute" Passion: "Conveying truth accurately and convincingly is one of the most important things I'll ever do." Objectivity: "If I'm wrong, I change course. I am open to reason. I want to *be* right; I don't just want to seem right or convince others I am."

STRIVE FOR THESE SUPERLATIVES. Be the kindest, most compassionate, most honest, most attentive, most well-researched, and most confident in the room. Be the one who cares most, who most seeks to uplift others, who is most prepared, and who is most thoughtful about the reason and logic and evidence behind the claims.

START BY CULTIVATING THE HIGHEST VIRTUES IN YOURSELF: love for your audience, love for truth, humility, a deep and abiding desire to make the world a better place, the desire to both be heard and to hear, and the desire to both teach and learn. You will find peace, purpose, clarity, confidence, and persuasive power.

START BY AVOIDING THESE TEMPTING MOTIVES. Avoid the desire to "outsmart" people, to overwhelm and dominate with your rhetorical strength, to embarrass your detractors, to win on the basis of cleverness alone, and to use words to attain power for its own sake. Don't set personal victory as your goal. Strive to achieve a victory for truth. And if you discover you are wrong, change course.

LISTEN TO YOURSELF TALK. (Peterson, 2018). See if what you are saying makes you feel stronger, physically, or weaker. If it makes you feel weaker, stop saying it. Reformulate your speech until you feel the ground under you solidifying.

SPEAK FROM A PLACE OF LOVE. It beats speaking from a desire to dominate. Our motivation and purpose in persuasion must be love. It's ethical *and* effective.

LOVE YOUR ENEMIES (OR HAVE NONE). If people stand against you, do not inflame the situation with resentment or anger. It does no good, least of all for you.

AVOID THESE CORRUPTING EMOTIONS: resistance, resentment, and anger. Against them, set acceptance, forgiveness, and love for all, even your enemies.

PLACE YOUR ATTENTION HERE, NOW. Be where you are. Attend to the moment. Forget the past. Forget the future. Nothing is more important than this.

FOCUS ON YOURSELF, BUT NOW. Speaking gurus will tell you to focus solely on your audience. Yes, that works. But so does focusing on yourself, as long as you focus on yourself *now*. Let this focus root you in the present. Don't pursue a mental commentary on what you see. Instead, just watch. Here. Now. No judgment.

ACCEPT YOUR FEAR. Everyone fears something. If you fear speaking, don't fear your fear of speaking too. Don't reprimand yourself for it. Accept it. Embrace it, even. Courage isn't action without fear. Courage is action despite fear.

STARE DOWN YOUR FEAR. To diminish your fear, stare at the object of your fear (and the fear itself), the way a boxer faces off with his opponent before the fight. Hold it in your mind, signaling to your own psyche that you can face your fear.

CHIP AWAY AT YOUR FEAR. The path out of fear is to take small, voluntary steps toward what you fear. Gradual exposure dissolves fear as rain carves stone.

LET THE OUTER SHAPE THE INNER. Your thoughts impact your actions. But your actions also impact your thoughts. To control fear, seek to manage its outward manifestations, and your calm exterior will shape your interior accordingly.

KNOW THAT EGO IS THE ENEMY. Ego is a black storm cloud blocking the warm sunlight of your true self. Ego is the creation of a false self that masquerades as your true self and demands gratification (which often manifests as the destruction of something good). The allure of arrogance is the siren-song of every good speaker. With it comes pride and the pursuit of power; a placing of the outer game before the inner. Don't fall for the empty promises of ego-gratification. Humility is power.

DON'T IDENTIFY WITH YOUR POSITIONS. Don't turn your positions into your psychological possessions. Don't imbue them with a sense of self.

NOTICE TOXIC AVATARS. When person A speaks to person B, they often craft a false idea, a false avatar, of both themselves and their interlocuter: A1 and B1. So does person B: B2 and A2. The resulting communication is a dance of false avatars; A1, B1, B2, and A2 communicate, but not person A and B. A false idea of one's self speaks to a false idea of someone else, who then does the same. This may be why George Bernard Shaw said "the greatest problem in communication is the illusion that it has been accomplished." How do you avoid this dance of false avatars? This conversation between concepts but not people? Be present. Don't prematurely judge. Let go of your *sense* of self, for just a moment, so your real self can shine forth.

MINE THE RICHES OF YOUR MIND. Look for what you need within yourself; your strengths and virtues. But also acknowledge and make peace with your own capacity for malevolence. Don't zealously assume the purity of your own motives.

RISE ABOVE YOUR MIND. The ability to think critically, reason, self-analyze, and self-criticize is far more important than being able to communicate, write, and speak. Introspect before you extrospect. Do not identify as your mind, but as the awareness eternally watching your mind. Do not be in your mind, but above it.

CLEAR THE FOG FROM YOUR PSYCHE. Know what you believe. Know your failures. Know your successes. Know your weaknesses. Know your strengths. Know what you fear. Know what you seek. Know your mind. Know yourself. Know your capacity for malevolence and evil. Know your capacity for goodness and greatness. Don't hide any part of yourself from yourself. Don't even try.

KNOW YOUR LOGOS. In 500 B.C. Heraclitus defined Logos as "that universal principle which animates and rules the world." What is your Logos? Meditate on it. Sit with it. Hold it up to the light, as a jeweler does with a gem, examining all angles.

KNOW YOUR LIMITS. The more you delineate and define the actions you consider unethical, the more likely you are to resist when they seem expedient.

REMEMBER THAT EVERYTHING MATTERS. There is no insignificant job, duty, role, mission, or speech. Everything matters. Everything seeks to beat back chaos in some way and create order. A laundromat doesn't deal in clean clothes, nor a trash disposal contractor in clean streets. They deal in order. In civilization. In human dignity. Don't ignore the reservoir of meaning and mattering upon which you stand. And remember that it is there, no matter where you stand.

GIVE THE GIFT OF MEANING. The greatest gift you can give to an audience is the gift of meaning; the knowledge that they matter, that they are irreplaceable.

HONOR YOUR INHERITANCE. You are the heir to thousands of years of human moralizing. Our world is shaped by the words of long-dead philosophers, and the gifts they gave us: gems of wisdom, which strengthen us against the dread and chaos of the world. We stand atop the pillars of 4,000 years of myth and meaning. Our arguments and moral compasses are not like planks of driftwood in a raging sea, but branches nourished by an inestimably old tree. Don't forget it.

BE THE PERSON YOU WANT TO BE SEEN AS. How do you want to be seen by your audience? How can you actually be that way, rather than just seeming to be?

HAVE TRUE ETHOS. Ethos is the audience's perception that the speaker has their best interests at heart. It's your job to make sure this perception is accurate.

CHANGE PLACES WITH YOUR AUDIENCE. Put yourself in their shoes, and then be the speaker you would want to listen to, the speaker worthy of your trust.

ACT AS THOUGH THE WHOLE WORLD IS WATCHING. Or as though a newspaper will publish a record of your actions. Or as though you're writing your autobiography with every action, every word, and even every thought. (You are).

ACT WITH AUDACIOUS HONOR. As did John McCain when he called Obama, his political opponent, "a decent family man, [and] citizen, that I just happen to have disagreements with." As did Socrates and Galileo when they refused to betray truth.

ADOPT A MECHANIC'S MENTALITY. Face your challenges the way a mechanic faces a broken engine; not drowning in emotion, but with objectivity and clarity. Identify the problem. Analyze the problem. Determine the solution. Execute the solution. If it works, celebrate. If not, repeat the cycle. This is true for both your inner and outer worlds: your fear of speaking, for example, is a specific problem with a specific fix, as are your destructive external rhetorical habits.

APPLY THE MASTERY PROCESS INTERNALLY. The four-step mastery process is not only for mastering your rhetoric, but also for striving toward internal mastery.

MARSHAL YOURSELF ALONG THE THREE AXES. To marshal means to place in proper rank or position – as in marshaling the troops – and to bring together and order in the most effective way. It is a sort of preparation. It begins with taking complete stock of what is available. Then, you order it. So, marshal yourself along three axes: the rhetorical axis (your points, arguments, rhetorical techniques, key phrases, etc.), the internal axis (your peace of mind, your internal principles, your mental climate, etc.), and the truth axis (your research, your facts, your logic, etc.).

PRACTICE ONE PUNCH 10,000 TIMES. As the martial arts adage says, "I fear not the man who practiced 10,000 punches once, but the man who practiced one punch 10,000 times." So it is with speaking skills and rhetorical techniques.

MULTIPLY YOUR PREPARATION BY TEN. Do you need to read a manuscript ten times to memorize it? Aim to read it 100 times. Do you need to research for one hour to grasp the subject of your speech? Aim to research for ten.

REMEMBER THE HIGHEST PRINCIPLE OF COMMUNICATION: the connection between speaker and audience – here, now – in this moment, in this place.

KNOW THERE'S NO SUCH THING AS A "SPEECH." All good communication is just conversation, with varying degrees of formality heaped on top. It's all just connection between consciousnesses. Every "difference" is merely superficial.

SEE YOURSELF IN OTHERS. What are you, truly? Rene Descartes came close to an answer in 1637, when he said "cogito, ego sum," I think therefore I am. The answer this seems to suggest is that your thoughts are most truly you. But your thoughts (and your character) change all the time. Something that never changes, arguably even during deep sleep, is awareness. Awareness is also the precondition for thought. A computer performs operations on information, but we don't say the computer "thinks." Why? Because it lacks awareness. So, I believe what makes you "you," most fundamentally, is your awareness, your consciousness. And if you accept this claim – which is by no means a mystical or religious one – then you must also see yourself in others. Because while the contents of everyone's consciousness is different, the consciousness itself is identical. How could it be otherwise?

FORGIVE. Yourself. Your mistakes. Your detractors. The past. The future. All.

FREE YOUR MIND. Many of the most challenging obstacles we face are thoughts living in our own minds. Identify these thoughts, and treat them like weeds in a garden. Restore the pristine poise of your mind, and return to equanimity.

LET. Let what has been be and what will be be. Most importantly, let what is be what is. Work to do what good you can do, and accept the outcome.

FLOW. Wikipedia defines a flow state as such: "a flow state, also known colloquially as being in the zone, is the mental state in which a person performing some activity is fully immersed in a feeling of energized focus, full involvement, and enjoyment in the process of the activity. In essence, flow is characterized by the complete absorption in what one does, and a resulting transformation in one's sense of time." Speaking in a flow state transports you and your audience outside of space and time. When I entered deep flow states during my speeches and debates, audience members would tell me that "it felt like time stopped." It felt that way for me too. Speaking in a flow state is a form of meditation. And it both leads to and results from these guidelines. Adhering to them leads to flow, and flow helps you adhere to them.

MEDITATE. Meditation brings your attention to the "here and now." It creates flow. Practice silence meditation, sitting in still silence and focusing on the motions of your mind, but knowing yourself as the entity watching the mind, not the mind itself. Practice aiming meditation, centering your noble aim in your mind, and focusing on the resulting feelings. (Also, speaking in flow is its own meditation).

EMBARK ON THE GRAND ADVENTURE. Take a place wherever you are. Develop influence and impact. Improve your status. Take on responsibility. Develop capacity and ability. Do scary things. Dare to leap into a high-stakes speech with no preparation if you must. Dare to trust your instincts. Dare to strive. Dare to lead. Dare to speak the truth freely, no matter how brutal it is. Be bold. Risk failure. Throw out your notes. The greatest human actions – those that capture our hearts and minds – occur on the border between chaos and order, where someone is daring to act and taking a chance when they know they could fall off the tightrope with no net below. Training wheels kill the sense of adventure. Use them if you need to, but only to lose them as soon as you can. Speak from the heart and trust yourself. Put yourself out there. Let people see the gears turning in your mind, let them see you grappling with your message in real time, taking an exploration in the moment. This is not an automaton doing a routine. It's not robotic or mechanical. That's too much order. It's also not unstructured nonsense. That's too much chaos. There is a risk of failure, mitigated not by training wheels, but by preparation. It is not a perfectly practiced routine, but someone pushing themselves just beyond their comfort zone, right at the cutting-edge of what they are capable of. It's not prescriptive. It's not safe either. The possibility that you could falter and fall in real-time calls out the best from you, and is gripping for the audience. It is also a thrilling adventure. Have faith in yourself, faith that you will say the right words when you need to. Don't think ahead, or backward. Simply experience the moment.

BREAK THE SEVEN LAWS OF WEAKNESS. If your goal is weakness, follow these rules. Seek to control what you can't control. Seek praise and admiration from others. Bend the truth to achieve your goals. Treat people as instruments in your game. Only commit to outer goals, not inner goals. Seek power for its own sake. Let anger and dissatisfaction fuel you in your pursuits, and pursue them frantically.

FAIL. Losses lead to lessons. Lessons lead to wins. If there's no chance of failure in your present task, you aren't challenging yourself. And if you aren't challenging yourself, you aren't growing. And that's the deepest and most enduring failure.

DON'T BETRAY YOURSELF. To know the truth and not say the truth is to betray the truth and to betray yourself. To know the truth, seek the truth, love the truth, and to speak the truth and speak it well, with poise and precision and power… this is to honor the truth, and to honor yourself. The choice is yours.

FOLLOW YOUR INNER LIGHT. As the Roman emperor and stoic philosopher Marcus Aurelius wrote in his private journal, "If thou findest in human life anything better than justice, truth, temperance, fortitude, and, in a word, anything better than thy own mind's self-satisfaction in the things which it enables thee to do according to right reason, and in the condition that is assigned to thee without thy own choice; if, I say, thou seest anything better than this, turn to it with all thy soul, and enjoy that which thou hast found to be the best. But if nothing appears to be better than [this], give place to nothing else." And as Kant said, treat humans as ends, not means.

JUDGE THEIR JUDGMENT. People *are* thinking of you. They *are* judging you. But what is their judgment to you? Nothing. (Compared to your self-judgment).

BREAK LESSER RULES IN THE NAME OF HIGHER RULES. Our values and moral priorities nest in a hierarchy, where they exist in relation to one another. Some are more important than others. If life compels a tradeoff between two moral principles, as it often does, this means there is a right choice. Let go the lesser of the two.

DON'T AVOID CONFLICT. Necessary conflict avoided is an impending conflict exacerbated. Slay the hydra when it has two heads, not twenty.

SEE THE WHOLE BOARD. Become wise in the ways of the world, and learned in the games of power and privilege people have been playing for tens of thousands of years. See the status-struggles and dominance-shuffling around you. See the chess board. But then opt to play a different game; a more noble game. The game of self-mastery. The game that transcends all other games. The worthiest game.

SERVE SOMETHING. Everyone has a master. Everyone serves something. Freedom is not the absence of service. Freedom is the ability to choose your service. What, to you, is worth serving? With your work and with your words?

TAKE RESPONSIBILITY FOR YOUR RIPPLE EFFECT. If you interact with 1,000 people, and they each interact with 1,000 more who also do the same, you are three degrees away from one billion people. Remember that compassion is contagious.

ONLY SPEAK WHEN YOUR WORDS ARE BETTER THAN SILENCE. And only write when your words are better than a blank page.

KNOW THERE IS THAT WHICH YOU DON'T KNOW YOU DON'T KNOW. Of course, there's that you know you don't know too. Recognize the existence of both of these domains of knowledge, which are inaccessible to you in your present state.

REMEMBER THAT AS WITHIN, SO (IT APPEARS) WITHOUT. If you orient your aim toward goals fueled by emotions like insecurity, jealousy, or vengeance, the world manifests itself as a difficult warzone. If you orient your aim toward goals fueled by emotions like universal compassion and positive ambition, the beneficence of the world manifests itself to you. Your aim and your values alter your perception.

ORIENT YOUR AIM PROPERLY. Actions flow from thought. Actions flow from *motives*. If you orient your aim properly – if you aim at the greatest good for the greatest number, at acting forthrightly and honorably – then this motive will fuel right actions, subconsciously, automatically, and without any forethought.

STOP TRYING TO USE SPEECH TO GET WHAT YOU WANT. Try to articulate what you believe to be true as carefully as possible, and then accept the outcome.

LEARN THE MEANING OF WHAT YOU SAY. Don't assume you already know.

USE THE MOST POWERFUL "RHETORICAL" TACTIC. There is no rhetorical tool more powerful than the overwhelming moral force of the unvarnished truth.

INJECT YOUR EXPERIENCE INTO YOUR SPEECH. Speak of what you know and testify of what you have seen. Attach your philosophizing and persuading and arguing to something real, some story you lived through, something you've seen.

DETACH FROM OUTCOME. As Stoic philosopher Epictetus said: "There is only one way to happiness and that is to cease worrying about things which are beyond the power of our will. Make the best use of what is in your power, and take the rest as it happens. The essence of philosophy is that a man should so live that his happiness shall depend as little as possible on external things. Remember to conduct yourself in life as if at a banquet. As something being passed around comes to you, reach out your hand and take a moderate helping. Does it pass you? Don't stop it. It hasn't yet come? Don't burn in desire for it, but wait until it arrives in front of you."

FOCUS ON WHAT YOU CONTROL. As Epictetus said, "It's not what happens to you, but how you react to it that matters. You may be always victorious if you will never enter into any contest where the issue does not wholly depend upon yourself. Some things are in our control and others not. Things in our control are opinion, pursuit, desire, aversion, and, in a word, whatever are our own actions. Things not in our control are body, property, reputation, command, and, in one word, whatever are not our own actions. Men are disturbed not by things, but by the view which they take of them. God has entrusted me with myself. Do not with that all things will go well with you, but that you will go well with all things." Before a high-stakes speech or event, I always tell myself this: "All I want from this, all I aim at, is to conduct what I control, my thoughts and actions, to the best of my ability. Any external benefit I earn is merely a bonus."

VIEW YOURSELF AS A VESSEL. Conduct yourself as something through which truth, brilliantly articulated, flows into the world; not as a self-serving entity, but a conduit for something higher. Speak not for your glory, but for the glory of good.

Want to Talk? Email Me:

PANDREIBUSINESS@GMAIL.COM

This is My Personal Email.
I Read Every Message and
Respond in Under 12 Hours.

Made in the USA
Las Vegas, NV
15 December 2023